EXE...
Sa...
Je...

MA...
Na...

CREATIVE DIRECTOR
Christine Ricks

PHOTOGRAPHER
BPD Studios

CONTRIBUTING PHOTOGRAPHERS
Heidi Stock, Lauren Dorton

VIDEOGRAPHER
Jake Doan

TECHNICAL WRITER
Edie McGinnis

TECHNICAL EDITOR
Jane Miller

PATTERN LAYOUT
Ally Simmons

PROJECT DESIGN TEAM
Natalie Earnheart, Jenny Doan,
Sarah Galbraith

AUTHOR OF THE FAIR THIEF
Steve Westover

CONTRIBUTING COPY WRITERS
Jenny Doan, Natalie Earnheart, Christine
Ricks, Katie Mifsud, Cammille Maddox,
Nichole Spravzoff

COPY EDITOR
Nichole Spravzoff

CONTRIBUTING PIECERS
Jenny Doan, Natalie Earnheart,
Carol Henderson, Cindy Morris

CONTRIBUTING QUILTERS
Jamey Stone-Quilting Department Manager,
Debbie Allen-Daytime Assistant Manager,
Kara Snow-Night Assistant Manager, Abby
Anderson, Betty Bates, Deloris Burnett,
Debbie Elder, James Evenson, Linda Frump,
Bernice Kelly, Sarah Richardson, Tory Wood,
Seth Wynne, Devin Ragle, Janet Caselman,
Karla Zinkand, Tonie Pew, Lynette Powers,
Rachel Hale, Angela Wilson, Michaela
Butterfield

PRINTING SERVICES
Walsworth Print Group
803 South Missouri
Marceline, MO 64658

CONTACT US
Missouri Star Quilt Company
114 N Davis
Hamilton, Mo. 64644
888-571-1122
info@missouriquiltco.com

content

Ooops! Sometimes we make mistakes.
To find corrections to every issue of Block
go to: www.msqc.co/corrections

hello
from MSQC

Summertime and the living is easy ... or is it? Well I guess it should be, but summertime for most of us is a season of work, not relaxation like when we were kids! It's time to get out there and mow, pull weeds, garden, and preserve all those berries we spent hours picking. There seems to be so much yard work to do that the quilting we love is often put on the back burner. When we do get to sew, it's in small bits of time that we steal back from our busy summer activities. But it's those sweet moments that keep us going until quilt season comes again, because quilting is our therapy! The best part of being a quilter in summer is that we get to see the fruits of our labors in full splendor. Nothing looks prettier than a beautiful quilt spread out on freshly mown grass or sparkling sand at the beach. Those quilts are just pictures waiting to happen. Sometimes when my family is gathered for a picnic and the kids are playing ball or flying a kite, I look out and survey the scene and it feels so surreal, too perfect, too good to be true. But then I realize these happy occasions are real and it takes my breath away. So in the picture perfect moments of summer—when it's finally warm, but not too hot—take a quilt out, toss it on the lawn, and just enjoy yourself.

JENNY DOAN
MISSOURI STAR QUILT CO

livin' it *UP!*

Summertime is a great excuse to roll out the patio furniture, clean off the BBQ, and spend some time outdoors. Who doesn't love lounging poolside with a popsicle in hand? These days are meant to be cherished. Warmer weather, delicious food, and get-togethers with friends and family makes summertime a wonderful opportunity to relax and focus on the simple things in life. It's so freeing to pay more attention to the beauty surrounding us that makes life even more enjoyable.

Lying on a quilt, looking up at the fluffy clouds floating by is my definition of living it up! This month's color co-op is full of all the things that remind me of summer: flowers, green grass, a bright picnic gingham, and lots of blues. Revel in the warmer days. Maybe try your hand at some paper piecing to pass the time while relaxing on those quilts you spent all winter making. Enjoy your summer—and if you find some lazy days ahead of you, pick up some fabric and do a little creating.

CHRISTINE RICKS
MSQC Creative Director, BLOCK MAGAZINE

SOLIDS

FBY12148 Bella Solids - Breeze by Moda Fabrics
SKU# 9900 132

FBY2514 Bella Solids - Cheddar by Moda Fabrics
SKU# 9900 152

FBY12155 Bella Solids - Azalea by Moda Fabrics
SKU# 9900 144

FBY3212 Bella Solids - Seafoam by Moda Fabrics
SKU# 9900 191

FBY1688 Bella Solids - Lime from Moda Fabrics
SKU #9900 75

FBY12203 Bella Solids - Cobalt by Moda Fabrics
SKU# 9900 227

PRINTS

FBY28595 Bloom and Bliss - Stripe Blue by Nadra Ridgeway of Ellis & Higgs for Riley Blake
SKU: C4585-BLUE

FBY11844 Lazy Day - Diamond Orange Yardage by Lori Whitlock for Riley Blake Designs
SKU: C3815-ORANGE

FBY39479 Carolina Gingham - ¼" Check Fuchsia by Robert Kaufman Fabrics for Robert Kaufman
SKU: P-16368-108

FBY16174 Hope Chest - Main Blue by Erin Turner for Penny Rose Designs
SKU: C4250-BLUE

FBY14407 Surprise! - Twist Green Yardage by Samantha Walker for Riley Blake Designs
SKU: C3955-GREEN

FBY21595 Summer Celebration - Stars Blue by Dani Mogstad for Riley Blake
SKU: C4444-BLUE

dresden botanica

quilt designed by JENNY DOAN

Some quilts are delicate antique heirlooms, meant to be admired more than used. They spend their long lives in cedar chests or carefully hung on the wall. They are true works of art, combining handiwork and love in one form. Some quilts are used and abused, dragged through the house by a toddler, made into blanket forts, grass stained, and napped on. And to me, those quilts are also marvelous works of art. Personally, I like to see a quilt getting some good use! Quilts are beautiful and useful. Don't be afraid to take one to the park and let it have a little fun.

Back in the day, we used to play a lively game we called "water balloon volleyball." We split up into two teams and each team held up the edges of a quilt. A water balloon was placed in the center of one of the loosely held quilts and then, at the count of 1-2-3, we pulled the quilt tight and sent the balloon shooting through the air! The other team's goal was to catch the balloon in their quilt. We got pretty good at the rhythm of catch-and-throw, but of course the best part of the game was when you missed the water balloon and it would burst on the ground, splashing everybody!

Of course you wouldn't use your great-grandmother's handstitched quilt for that game, but every quilt has it's own

For the tutorial and everything need you to make this quilt visit:
www.msqc.co/blocksummer16

beauty and purpose. Over the years, I've gained a strong appreciation for the heirloom quilts that had been left behind by previous generations. In the early days of Missouri Star Quilt Company, many of the quilts I worked on had been pieced by the mothers and grandmothers of my customers. It was such a special privilege to transform quilt tops from generations past into finished quilts that, after years of storage, could finally be used and enjoyed.

When we first opened up shop in 2008, we offered machine quilting services along with a few shelves of fabric. In a town of less than 2,000, however, business was scarce. Our friends and neighbors tried their best to support us, but most of them weren't even quilters. Lucky for me, many of them had held onto unfinished projects, long forgotten in storage closets and cedar chests. Pretty soon these old quilts started rolling in, and I had a ball quilting antique works of art.

A good number of those old quilt tops were Dresden Plates, and I just couldn't get over how beautiful they were. I absolutely fell in love with those perfect little "petals," but I was too intimidated to try to make one myself.

When I finally gathered up the courage, I decided to make my own Dresden Plate quilt out of reproduction 1930's fabric, and was delighted to discover how easy it was. With just a little ingenuity, a special ruler, and a charm pack, my first Dresden came together in a jiffy!

Since that time, I've become obsessed with the Dresden Plate pattern and I see them everywhere! One year I made

a Thanksgiving turkey with Dresden feathers, then I made a Christmas tree hanging with green Dresden branches. I've also made several spring wall hangings with Dresden flowers. So just remember, if you want something bad enough, it is possible and you can do it one seam at a time!

One of the great joys of quilting is knowing that I am creating something that will be cherished and enjoyed long after this moment has become a distant memory. Take time to make something today and you'll leave a lasting legacy.

materials

makes a 65" X 78½" quilt

QUILT TOP
- 6 packages 5" squares
- 3 yards 42" wide background fabric

BORDER
- 1½ yards

BINDING
- ¾ yard

BACKING
- 4¾ yards

ADDITIONAL SUPPLIES
- MSQC Dresden Plate Template
- 1 cardboard circle template cut from the template given on pg. 15. *Be sure your template matches the "inner circle" line.*

SAMPLE QUILT
- **Bread and Butter** by American Jane for Moda

1 cut

From the 5" squares, cut:

- 400 wedges using the Dresden Plate Template.

- 20 circles matching the perimeter of the outer circle shown on the template on pg. 15.

From the background fabric, cut:

- (7) 14" wide strips across the width of the fabric – Subcut the strips into 14" squares for a total of **20 squares.**

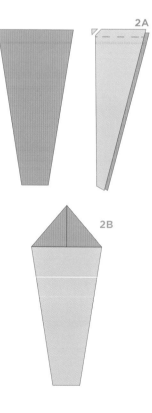

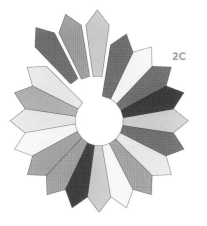

2C

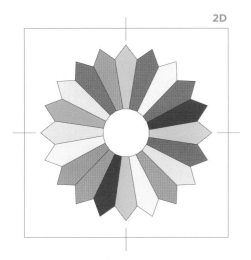

2D

2E

2 sew

Fold 1 wedge in half lengthwise, with right sides facing. Stitch straight across the larger end. **2A**

Trim the corner, open the seam and turn the point right side out. Press, centering the seam. **Make 400. 2B**

Join 20 wedges to make a Dresden Plate. Begin sewing at the top of the wedge and stop at the bottom. **2C**

Lightly press 1 background 14″ square in quarters to make placement lines. Using the creases as a guide, center a Dresden Plate on a square. Pin in place. **2D**

Make a gathering stitch around 1 circle about ⅛″ in from the edge. Place the inner circle template on the wrong side of the circle and pull the thread to gather. Press the circle and remove the template.

Center the prepared circle on the Dresden plate and pin in place.

Appliqué the plate and the circle to the background square to complete the block. **Make 20. 2E**

Block Size: 13½″ x 13½″ finished

3 arrange in rows

Lay out the blocks in **5 rows** with each row having **4 blocks.** When you are happy with the arrangement, sew the blocks together. Press the seam allowances of rows 1, 3, 5 toward the left and the remaining rows toward the right. This will make it easier to make your seams nest and line up. Sew the rows together.

4 border

Cut (7) 6″ strips across the width of the fabric. Sew the strips together end-to-end to make one long strip. Trim the borders from this strip.

Refer to Borders (pg. 100) in the Construction Basics to measure and cut the outer borders. The strips are approximately 68″ for the sides and approximately 65½″ for the top and bottom.

5 quilt and bind

Layer the quilt with batting and backing and quilt. After the quilting is complete, square up the quilt and trim away all excess batting and backing. Add binding to complete the quilt. See Construction Basics (pg. 101) for binding instructions.

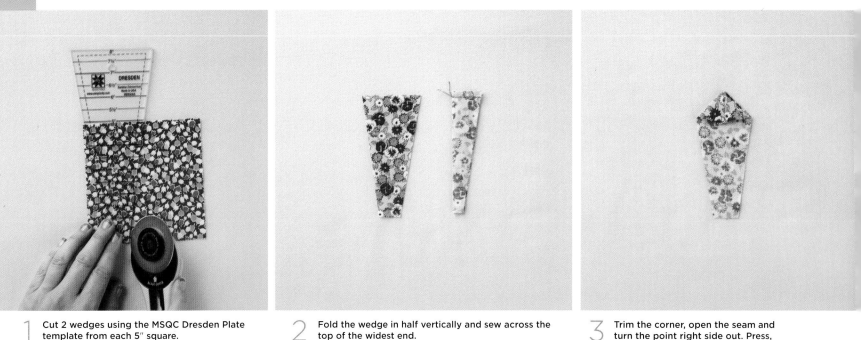

1   Cut 2 wedges using the MSQC Dresden Plate template from each 5″ square.

2   Fold the wedge in half vertically and sew across the top of the widest end.

3   Trim the corner, open the seam and turn the point right side out. Press, centering the seam.

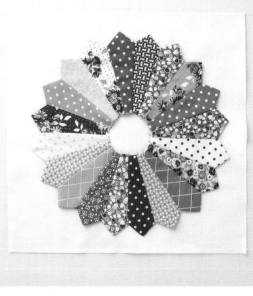

4   Sew 20 wedges together.

5   Center the plate on a background square and pin in place.

6   Appliqué the block and the center circle to the background square to complete the block.

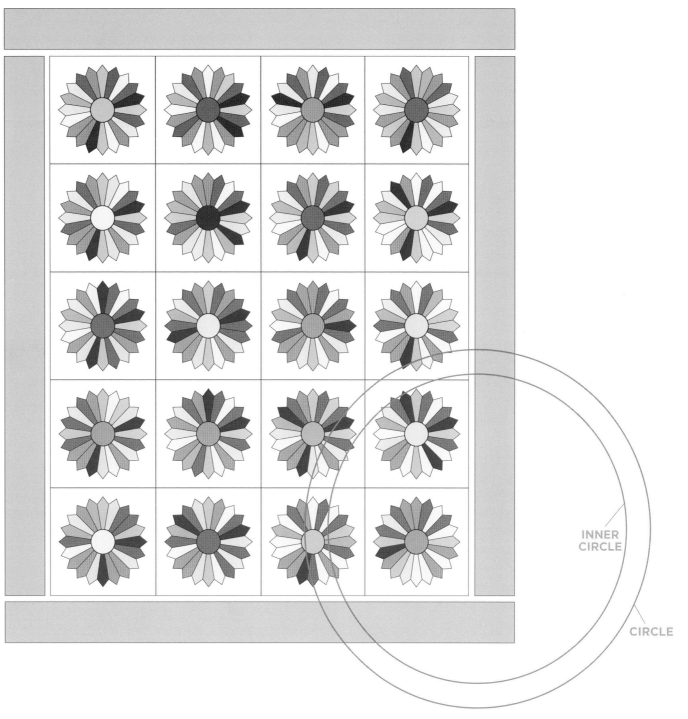

INNER
CIRCLE

CIRCLE

I spy jar

quilt designed by JENNY DOAN

One of our favorite movies at the Doan house is *Chitty Chitty Bang Bang.* I'm sure we watched it a hundred times when the kids were small, and there isn't a line or lyric we can't all recite by heart! And, oh, how the kids dreamed of riding in that magical car that could navigate land, sea, and sky to carry them away on far-off adventures!

When you're on hour seven of a twelve hour road trip, a magical flying car like *Chitty Chitty Bang Bang* would solve all your problems. Tensions are running high and your little darlings have had about as much togetherness as they can handle. Shrieks of "Mom! She's touching me!" and "Mom! He ate all the Cheetos!" are ringing in your ears, and even a twelve passenger van can't provide enough space for seven wiggly kids and two frazzled parents to travel in peace.

That's when you break out the tried and true game of I Spy. It's simple in concept, but very effective in calming a group of rowdy kids. This game is a life saver. The beauty of I Spy is that it can be played anywhere. Children of all ages can join in on the fun, and everyone gets a turn. When the kids were tiny, the game was always simple, and half of the time the item

For the tutorial and everything you need to make this quilt visit.
www.msqc.co/blocksummer16

being spied was the blue sky! As the kids grew older, however, things got pretty competitive, but we always had a great time no matter how serious the game.

When I first became interested in quilting, one of the quilts I really wanted to make was an I Spy quilt. I spent hours in the local fabric shop searching for interesting prints to add to my quilt like taxi cabs, football helmets, dancing hotdogs, pink flamingos, anything that would make for a fun game of I Spy. It's so much easier now that fabric companies offer I Spy bundles. I can just pick up a pack and start sewing!

Now that I'm a grandma, I've made I Spy quilts for many of my grandchildren, and there's nothing like cuddling up with your favorite little people for a story and a quick game of I Spy. It's such a simple thing, but simple things often make the very best memories.

Some years have passed and our dream has actually come true; the kids surprised their dad with an old 1926 Ford Model T! We were delighted to finally have our very own "pretty Chitty Bang Bang." It's not quite up to long road trips, but Ron has had a wonderful time puttering with that old car, and just recently he actually got it running, although we're still waiting on flying and seafaring capabilities!

Sometimes I miss those days when we used to take road trips together as a family, but when I hop in the Model T with Ron, accompanied by a grandkid or two, I smile as we drive slowly along the familiar roads in our hometown, waving to friends we see along the way.

 Here's another colorway of this block. Try different combinations of fabric to see which one you like best.

materials

makes a 50" X 63½" quilt

QUILT TOP
- 1 package 5" squares (42 ct.)
- ¼ yard solid (lids)
- 2 yards background (includes inner border)

BORDER
- 1 yard

BINDING
- ¾ yard

BACKING
- 4 yards

SAMPLE QUILT
- **I Spy - It's A Boy Thing** by Timeless Treasures

1 cut

From the solid fabric, cut:

- (2) 3" strips across the width of the fabric.

From the background fabric, cut:

- (10) 1½" strips across the width of the fabric – Set aside 4 strips and subcut the remaining 6 strips into 1½" squares for a **total of 168.**

- (12) 2½" strips across the width of the fabric – Subcut 6 of the strips into 2½" x 6" rectangles for a **total of 35.** Set aside for sashing rectangles. Reserve the remaining strips for horizontal sashing.

2B

2 sew

On the reverse side of the background 1½" squares, draw a line from corner to corner once on the diagonal. This line is your sewing line. 2A

Place a marked 1½" background square on one corner of a print 5" square with right sides facing. Sew on the marked line. Trim ¼" away from the sewn line. Press the triangle toward the outside of the print. Repeat for the remaining 3 corners. **Make 42 "jars."** 2B

3 make strip set

Sew a 1½" strip to either side of a 3" solid strip. Press the seam allowances toward the darker fabric. Make 2 and cut each strip set into 1½" increments. You need a **total of 42** to use as lids for the jars. 3A

4 sew

Sew a strip set "lid" to the top of each "jar" to complete the blocks. **You will have 42.** 4A

Block Size: 4½" x 5½" finished

5 lay out blocks

Arrange your blocks in **7 rows** with each row having **6 blocks.**

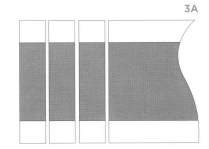

3A

4A

When you are satisfied with the arrangement, begin sewing the blocks together, adding a 2½" x 6" sashing rectangle between the blocks as shown. 5A

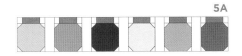

5A

Measure the rows from side to side (approximately 37½"). Trim 6 sashing strips to your measurement. Stitch a sashing strip between each row. Refer to the assembly diagram if necessary.

6 inner border

Cut (5) 2½" strips across the width of the fabric. Sew the strips together end-to-end to make one long strip. Trim the borders from this strip.

Refer to Borders (pg. 100) in the Construction Basics to measure and cut the inner borders. The strips are approximately 51" for the sides and approximately 41½" for the top and bottom.

7 outer border

Cut (6) 5" strips across the width of the fabric. Sew the strips together end-to-end to make one long strip. Trim the borders from this strip.

Refer to Borders (pg. 100) in the Construction Basics to measure and cut the outer borders. The strips are approximately 55" for the sides and approximately 50½" for the top and bottom.

8 quilt and bind

Layer the quilt with batting and backing and quilt. After the quilting is complete, square up the quilt and trim away all excess batting and backing. Add binding to complete the quilt. See Construction Basics (pg. 101) for binding instructions.

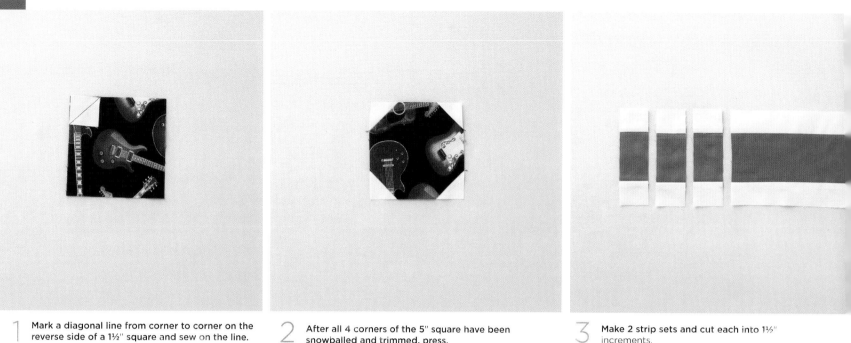

1   Mark a diagonal line from corner to corner on the reverse side of a 1½″ square and sew on the line. Trim ¼″ away from the outside of the sewn seam.

2   After all 4 corners of the 5″ square have been snowballed and trimmed, press.

3   Make 2 strip sets and cut each into 1½″ increments.

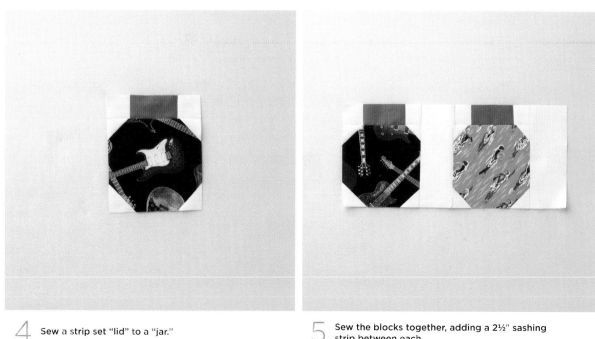

4   Sew a strip set "lid" to a "jar."

5   Sew the blocks together, adding a 2½″ sashing strip between each.

BONUS PROJECT: WALL HANGING

materials
makes a 29½" X 35" wall hanging

WALL HANGING
- (6) 5" x 10" print rectangles
- (1) 3" x 10" strip of solid (lids)
- ¾ yard background – includes inner border

OUTER BORDER
- ¾ yard

BACKING
- 1¼ yard

BINDING
- ½ yard

SAMPLE QUILT
- **Farmer's Market** collection by RJR

1 cut
From the background fabric, cut

- (2) 1½" strips across the width of the fabric – Subcut 1 strip into (24) 1½" squares. Subcut the remaining strip into (2) 1½" x 10" rectangles. Set aside the remaining fabric for sashing and the inner border.

2 sew
On the reverse side of the background 1½" squares, draw a line from corner to corner once on the diagonal. This line is your sewing line. **2A**

Place a marked 1½" background square on one corner of a print 5" x 10"

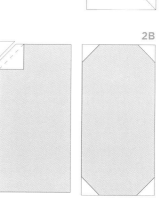

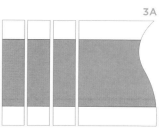

rectangle with right sides facing. Sew on the marked line. Trim ¼" away from the sewn line. Press the triangle toward the outside of the print. Repeat for the remaining 3 corners. **Make 6 "jars."** 2B

3 make a strip set

Sew a 1½" x 10" rectangle to either side of the 3" x 10" solid strip. Press the seam allowances toward the darker fabric. Cut the strip set into 1½"

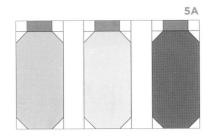

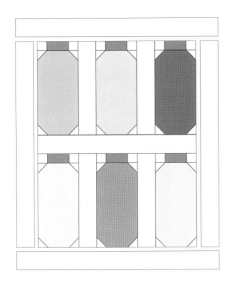

5A

increments. You need a **total of 6** to use as lids for the jars. 3A

4 sew

Sew a strip set "lid" to the top of each "jar" to complete the blocks. **You will have 6.** 4A

Cut Sashing Strips

- (2) 2½" strips across the width of the fabric – subcut 1 strip into (3) 2½" x 11" rectangles and cut (1) 2½" x 11" rectangle and (1) 2½" x 18" rectangle. Set the remaining fabric aside for the inner border.

5 lay out blocks

Arrange your blocks in **2 rows** with each row having **3 blocks.** Sew the blocks together, adding a 2½" x 11" sashing rectangle between the blocks as shown. 5A

Measure the rows from side to side (approximately 18"). Sew the 2½" x 18" sashing rectangle between the 2 rows.

6 inner border

Cut (4) 2½" strips across the width of the fabric. Refer to Borders (pg. 100) in the Construction Basics to measure and trim the inner borders. The strips are approximately 23½" for the sides and approximately 22" for the top and bottom.

7 outer border

Cut (4) 4½" strips across the width of the fabric. Refer to Borders (pg. 100) in the Construction Basics to measure and trim the outer borders. The strips are approximately 27½" for the sides and approximately 30" for the top and bottom.

Layer the quilt with batting and backing and quilt. After the quilting is complete, square up the quilt and trim away all excess batting and backing. Add binding to complete the quilt. See Construction Basics (page 101) for binding instructions.

For the tutorial and everything you need to make this quilt visit:
www.msqc.co/blocksummer16

stacks
quilt

quilt designed by JENNY DOAN

Reading can take you anywhere you want to go! Books are absolutely amazing. They have the power to transport us without even leaving the room. From adventures to mysteries and beyond, I have always loved reading. I'm happy to say that this trait has been passed down through my children to my grandchildren. We love cuddling up together with a big stack of books. It's easy to lose track of time reading together, and maybe bedtime gets pushed back just a little. But that's our secret!

My nightstand is usually teetering under a tall stack of books from the secondhand store, just waiting for me to dive in and read to my heart's content. I always read before bed to get my mind to turn off and relax. My favorite stories take me to a place where I can leave work behind and drift off to sleep. I love reading, and I have so many sweet memories of sharing books with my loved ones.

When the kids were small, I had a habit of reading to them every day after lunch. With peanut butter and jelly on their little faces, they'd rest their heads on their hands and listen to book after book. We reveled in the creative ways Mrs. Piggle Wiggle got kids to obey or the silly mixups our friend Amelia Bedelia had just trying to bake a cake! They joke that I read until either they fell asleep or I did! Now, a generation later, I love to hear my grown-up children gather their own kids together and read them a story. It is such a wonderful sound as the normally boisterous bunch gets quieter and waits with bated breath to hear what comes next.

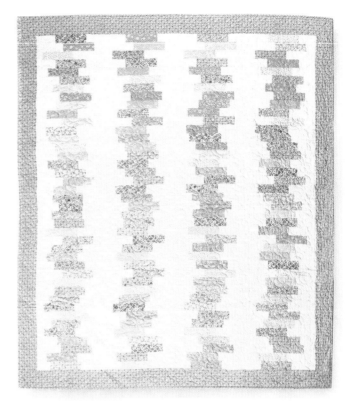

Reading to children is wonderful for their young minds, and I've heard that it's beneficial to begin reading with babies as young as possible. Even if they don't understand a word, when you read to a little one cradled in your arms, you're teaching them to associate reading with closeness, warmth, and love. What a beautiful way to teach a child! One of the most tender sights I've ever seen was my own mother holding one of her new great-grandbabies as she read a sweet story with the three year-old sister. A love of reading is one of the best gifts we can give our children.

I like to think that a love of reading runs in families, and around here we're definitely hooked.

“ Even if they don't understand a word, when
you read to a little one cradled in your arms,
you're teaching them to associate reading with
closeness, warmth, and love. ”

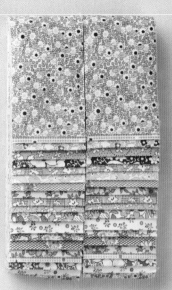

materials

makes a 76½" X 89" quilt

QUILT TOP
- 1 roll print 2½" strips
- 1 roll background strips

BORDER
- 1½ yards

BINDING
- ¾ yard

BACKING
- 7 yards

SAMPLE QUILT
- **Pinafores and Petticoats** by Kaye England for Wilmington Prints

1 cut

Cut each of the print strips into (4) 8" rectangles.

Cut each of the background strips into (4) 10" rectangles.

2 sew

Beginning with a background rectangle, sew 4 background rectangles and 4 print rectangles together, alternating the background pieces with the prints into one strip. **Make 40. 2A**

Sew each strip into a loop.

Cut the loop in two on a background rectangle, staying at least approximately 2" from the seam line. Instead of measuring, cut at random intervals to gain the staggered effect. If you find the stacks appear to be leaning more in one direction than another, flip the strip around. **2B**

Lay out the rows and sew them together once you are satisfied with the layout.

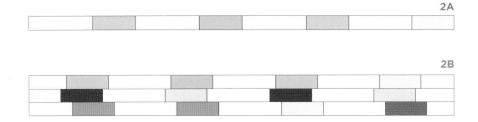

2A

2B

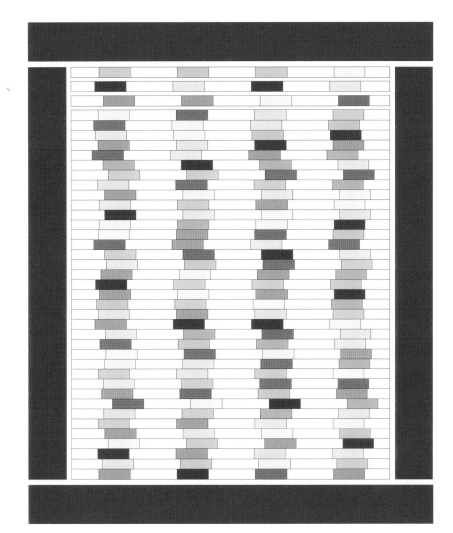

3 border

Cut (8) 5" strips across the width of the fabric. Sew the strips together end-to-end to make one long strip. Trim the borders from this strip.

Refer to Borders (pg. 100) in the Construction Basics to measure and cut the outer borders. The strips are approximately 80½" for the sides and approximately 77" for the top and bottom.

4 binding

Layer the quilt with backing and batting and quilts as desired. Square up and trim the excess batting and backing away. Add binding to finish. See the Construction Basics (pg. 101) for binding instructions.

For the tutorial and everything
you need to make this quilt visit:
www.msqc.co/blocksummer16

summer
in the park

quilt designed by NATALIE EARNHEART

In towns and cities across the globe, local parks are the heart of the community. Imaginations run free, friendships thrive, and memories are made that will last a lifetime. We live such busy lives, it's so important to have a place where we can spend time enjoying the moment. Thank goodness for the park! When my children were young, they were always begging to go to the park and play. We loved to pack up a picnic and spend the whole afternoon relaxing in the sunshine.

Nowadays, we still love to hang out in the park, especially when the weather warms up. Here in Hamilton, we gather together as a community in good ol' Penney Park. We may not have the bustling nightlife of the big city, but we know how to have a good time! With farmer's markets, JC Penney

Days, parades, fireworks, and Friday night football games at the high school, there's a lot of fun to be had. When you only have a couple thousand folks in town, there's plenty of room for everyone, and you never have to fight for a parking spot.

Best of all, if you roll into our town on a warm summer night, you just might be lucky enough to stumble upon Movies in the Park, one of our favorite Hamilton traditions. All it takes is a big blow-up screen, a projector, and a quilt to lie on under the stars, and you have the makings of a completely magical evening!

Folks start to arrive at the park late in the afternoon to spread out their quilts and grab some dinner from the food stands. Music plays and the savory aroma of freshly grilled burgers and buttery popcorn wafts through the air, giving the whole scene a festive atmosphere. We sit and gab with friends and neighbors as the day fades into night. Then it's time to settle down and watch the show. It doesn't seem to matter what's playing, all that matters is that we're together. Sometimes, as the lightning bugs dance through the cool evening air, I can't help but look around at all my friends and neighbors and think how lucky I am to live in a small town.

materials

makes a 74" x 81¾" quilt

QUILT TOP
- 1 roll of 2½" print strips
- 1 roll of 2½" background strips

INNER BORDER
- ¾ yard

OUTER BORDER AND BINDING
- 1¾ yards

BACKING
- 5 yards

SAMPLE QUILT
- **Blossom Batiks Jewel Tones** by Flaurie & Finch for RJR

1 make strip sets

Strip Set A
Sew a print 2½" strip to either side of a 2½" background strip. Press the seam allowances toward the prints. **Make 13. 1A**

Strip Set B
Sew a background 2½" strip to either side of a print 2½" strip. Press the seam allowances toward the print. **Make 13. 1B**

2 block construction

Place 1 *Strip Set A* atop 1 *Strip Set B* with right sides facing. Stitch the

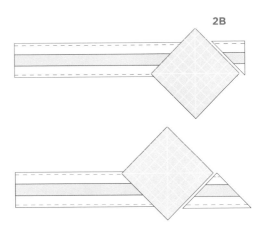

2B

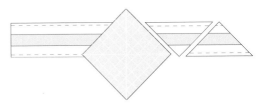

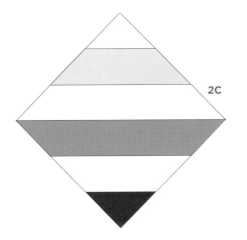

2C

2 together by sewing the 2 long edges together using a ¼" seam allowance. When you have finished, you will have a tube. **Make 13 tubes.** 2A

Place a 12½" square ruler on a tube unit with the marked diagonal 45-degree center line resting on the sewn seam. Cut away the end piece and flip the ruler so the diagonal center line is on the opposite seam line. Cut 1 pieced triangle. Continue cutting the tube units in this manner to make **72 pieced triangles.** 2B

Press each pieced triangle block open. 2C

Block Size: 7¾" x 7¾"

3 lay out in rows

Lay out the blocks in rows. Each row is made up of **8 blocks** across and you need **9 rows.** Refer to the assembly diagram and turn each block in the direction indicated.

When you are happy with the layout, sew the blocks together into rows, then sew the rows together.

4 inner border

Cut (8) 2½" strips across the width of the fabric. Sew the strips together end-to-end to make one long strip. Trim the borders from this strip.

Refer to Borders (pg. 100) in the Construction Basics to measure and cut the inner borders. The strips are approximately 70¼" for the sides and approximately 66½" for the top and bottom.

5 outer border

Cut (8) 4½" strips across the width of the fabric. Sew the strips together end-to-end to make one long strip. Trim the borders from this strip.

Refer to Borders (pg. 100) in the Construction Basics to measure and cut the outer borders. The strips are approximately 74¼" for the sides and approximately 74½" for the top and bottom.

6 quilt and bind

Layer the quilt with batting and backing and quilt. After the quilting is complete, square up the quilt and trim away all excess batting and backing. Add binding to complete the quilt. See Construction Basics (pg. 101) for binding instructions.

1   To make strip set A, sew a 2½" print strip to either side of a background strip.

2   Make strips set B by sewing a 2½" background strip to either side of a 2½" print strip.

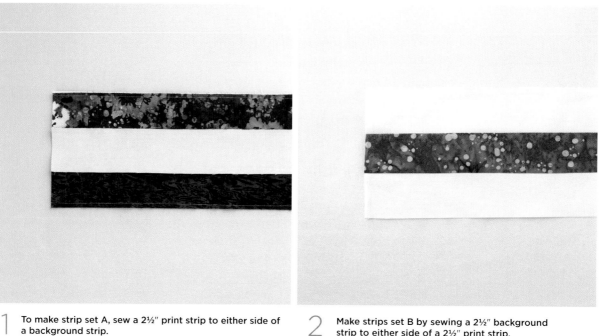

3   Using a 12½" square ruler, place the marked 45-degree line on the sewn seam and cut triangles. Refer to diagram 2B on page 37, if necessary.

4   Open the block and press.

5   Turn the blocks as necessary to match the layout on page 39.

For the tutorial and everything you need to make this quilt visit:
www.msqc.co/blocksummer16

rhombus
cube

quilt designed by NATALIE EARNHEART

As our family grows up, so do our adventures. I no longer pull the kids through town in a wagon, but we still like to get together and have fun. My kids have graduated from tricycles to motorcycles, and I couldn't be prouder. My daughter, Sarah, has a great farmhouse just outside of town with its own pond and plenty of space to run around, or in our case, to ride around.

I absolutely love watching my kids ride motorcycles together. We have a few mini bikes that they all take turns riding and sometimes they like to play a game we call "motorcycle soccer." In this game you have to strike the perfect balance between staying on your bike and moving the ball, kicking it alongside the motorcycle. It's hilarious to watch! We could be on any blooper TV show and take the cake.

The excitement begins with a kind of kickoff—all the bikes circle up around a soccer ball, engines revving, and then, they're off! It's a bit of chaos and a lot of fun! By the end of the game, everyone's covered in mud and grass, with big smiles on their faces.

We've never been afraid of a little dirt in this family. Often our favorite games are simple ones. When the kids were little, we used to find a nice rounded, grassy hill and spend hours racing up to the top, lying on our sides, and rolling like a log down to the bottom. Grass stains and scraped knees were just a part of life. I like to keep things simple, if I can, and quilting, much like life, can be as simple or as complicated as we allow it to be.

One way of keeping things simple is looking at a problem in a new way. Instead of struggling to go up and over a challenge, why not just go around? With this pattern we wondered, "is it possible to create a rhombus cube without a Y-seam?" By using triangles along with the rhombus shape, those pesky Y-seams are completely eliminated! If you've been avoiding a Tumbling Blocks pattern for some time, now you can relax and give the Rhombus quilt a try. Allow yourself to unwind and simplify your life—and don't worry about grass stains on your knees. We don't mind.

materials

makes an 80" X 80¾" quilt

QUILT TOP
- 2 yards light
- 2 yards medium
- 2 yards dark
- 1½ yards solid (we used gray) - includes yardage for border

BACKING
- 7½ yards

BINDING
- ¾ yard

OTHER SUPPLIES
- MSQC Rhombus Template

SAMPLE QUILT
- **Kona Solids: Titanium** K00-500, **Pool** K00-45 *OR* **Azure** K00-1009, **Nightfall** K00-140, **Aqua** K00-1005

1 cut

From the light fabric, cut:

- (12) 5" strips across the width of the fabric – subcut the strips into **72 rhombuses.**

From the medium fabric, cut:

- (12) 5" strips across the width of the fabric – subcut the strips into **72 rhombuses.**

From the dark fabric, cut:

- (12) 5" strips across the width of the fabric – subcut the strips into **144 triangles.**

2A

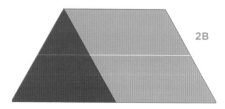

2B

2C   2D

A ROW   B ROW

From the border fabric, cut:

- (3) 5″ strips across the width of the fabric – subcut the strips into **32 triangles.**

2 sew

Sew a dark triangle onto the end of a light rhombus as shown. **Make 72.** 2A

Sew a dark triangle onto the end of a medium rhombus as shown. **Make 72.** 2B

For this quilt, we are going to sew our rows together vertically. Begin and end each row with a gray triangle. Refer to diagram 2C and sew the triangles and rhombuses together as shown. Notice that after the initial gray triangle, the row begins with a dark triangle and is followed by a light rhombus going from top to bottom. Pay particular attention to color placement. We'll call these A rows. **Make 8.** 2C

Again, begin and end each row with a gray triangle. Refer to diagram 2D and sew the triangles and rhombuses together as shown. Notice that after the initial gray triangle, the row begins with a dark triangle followed by a medium rhombus going from top to bottom. Pay particular attention to color placement. We'll call these B rows. **Make 8.** 2D

Sew the rows together, alternating the A rows with the B rows. Press the A rows in one direction and the B rows in the opposite to make your seams nest. 2E

After the rows are sewn together, trim the top and bottom edges evenly with the rhombus and medium triangles. Be sure you leave a ¼″ seam allowance as you trim. 2F

3 border

Cut (8) 4½″ strips across the width of the fabric. Sew the strips together end-to-end to make one long strip. Trim the borders from this strip.

Refer to Borders (pg. 100) in the Construction Basics to measure and cut the outer borders. The strips are approximately 73¼″ for the sides and approximately 80½″ for the top and bottom.

2E

2F

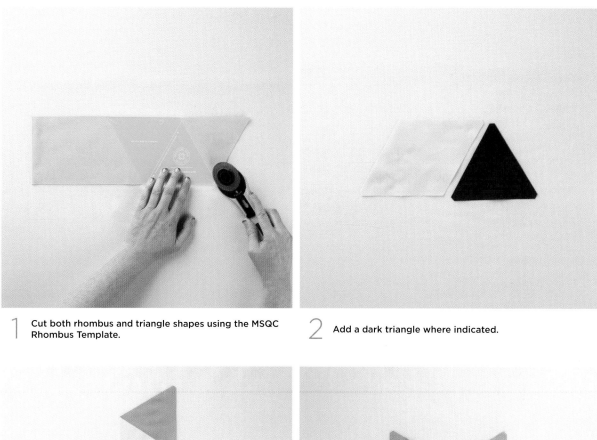

1 Cut both rhombus and triangle shapes using the MSQC Rhombus Template.

2 Add a dark triangle where indicated.

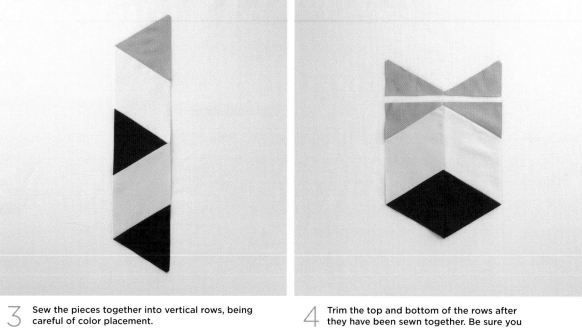

3 Sew the pieces together into vertical rows, being careful of color placement.

4 Trim the top and bottom of the rows after they have been sewn together. Be sure you leave ¼" seam allowance as you trim.

4 quilt and bind

Layer the quilt with batting and backing and quilt. After the quilting is complete, square up the quilt and trim away all excess batting and backing. Add binding to complete the quilt. See Construction Basics (pg. 101) for binding instructions.

For the tutorial and everything you need to make this quilt visit:
www.msqc.co/blocksummer16

jelly basket

quilt designed by JENNY DOAN

I was a little girl when the movie *Mary Poppins* came out. It's the only time I remember my whole family going to the movies together. We all piled into the car and drove to Monterey to the theater. Even my Dad went; it was a big deal! From start to finish, I was enthralled! I loved the whole show, every part of it, and I have watched it over and over throughout the years.

There are so many things to love about *Mary Poppins* and when I was a kid I felt so drawn to the scenes where they jumped into cartoon sketches and magically cleaned the nursery with just a snap, but it wasn't until I watched the movie as an adult that I really began to understand the message. There's quite a bit of fun to be had, but underlying those moments, there's a genuine

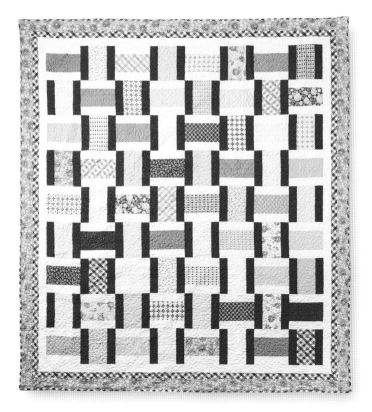

struggle taking place in the Banks family. The children are hoping for their parents to have more time for them. And Mary knew just how to help Mr. and Mrs. Banks see the importance of spending time together as a family.

In the final scene, Mr. Banks finally leaves the pressures of his career behind for a moment and takes the kids away to go fly kites. It's a simple act, but it communicates so much. I feel the weight of the world lifted off of my shoulders when I can focus on the simple joys of life. Showing the people around you that you love them is not a complicated act, but it takes time and patience.

When I get too stressed or busy, I remind myself of a song I have loved since that trip to the movies so many years ago. The words "Let's go fly a kite and send it soaring!" mean so much more now. Especially if we have little people around, something as small as flying a kite together can make their day. Take time for the people you love and your heart will soar!

materials
makes an 81" X 89" quilt

QUILT TOP
- 1 package 10" squares
- 2 yards light solid – includes inside border
- 1½ yards dark solid

MIDDLE BORDER
- ¾ yard

OUTER BORDER
- 1 yard

BINDING
- ¾ yard

BACKING
- 7½ yards

SAMPLE QUILT
- **Summerfest** by April Rosenthal for Moda

1 cut

Select 36 squares from the package. Cut each in half to make 5" x 10" rectangles.

From the light solid, cut:

- (18) 2½" strips across the width of the fabric – subcut the strips into 2½" x 10" rectangles for a **total of 72.** Set the remaining fabric aside for the inside border.

From the dark solid, cut:

- (18) 2½" strips across the width of the fabric – subcut the strips into 2½" x 10" rectangles for a **total of 72.**

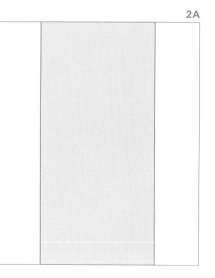

2A

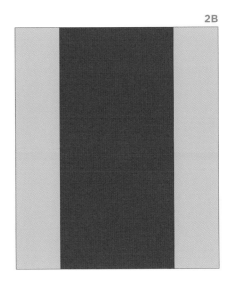

2B

2C

2 sew

Sew a light solid 2½" x 10" strip on either side of a print 5" x 10" rectangle. **Make 36.** 2A

Sew a dark solid 2½" x 10" strip on either side of a print 5" x 10" rectangle. **Make 36.** 2B

Trim each block to a 9" square. 2C

Block Size: 8½" x 8½" finished

3 lay out blocks

Lay out the blocks in rows. Each row will have **8 blocks** and you need **9 rows.** The light bordered blocks and the dark bordered blocks will alternate. Refer to the assembly diagram for placement.

When you are happy with the placement of your blocks, sew the blocks together. Press the seam allowances of rows 1, 3, 5, 7, and 9 toward the left and the remaining rows, toward the right.

Sew the rows together.

4 inner border

Cut (8) 2½" strips across the width of the fabric. Sew the strips together end-to-end to make one long strip. Trim the borders from this strip.

Refer to Borders (pg. 100) in the Construction Basics to measure and cut the inner borders. The strips are approximately 77" for the sides and approximately 72½" for the top and bottom.

5 middle border

Cut (9) 2" strips across the width of the fabric. Sew the strips together end-to-end to make one long strip. Trim the borders from this strip.

Refer to Borders (pg. 100) in the Construction Basics to measure and cut the inner borders. The strips are approximately 81" for the sides and approximately 75½" for the top and bottom.

6 outer border

Cut (9) 3½" strips across the width of the fabric. Sew the strips together end-to-end to make one long strip. Trim the borders from this strip.

Refer to Borders (pg. 100) in the Construction Basics to measure and cut the outer borders. The strips are approximately 84" for the sides and approximately 81½" for the top and bottom.

7 quilt and bind

Layer the quilt with batting and backing and quilt. After the quilting is complete, square up the quilt and trim away all excess batting and backing. Add binding to complete the quilt. See Construction Basics (pg. 101) for binding instructions.

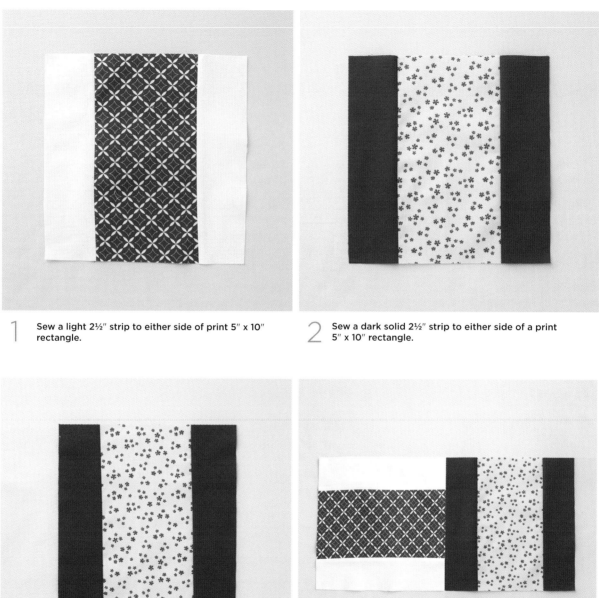

1 Sew a light 2½″ strip to either side of print 5″ x 10″ rectangle.

2 Sew a dark solid 2½″ strip to either side of a print 5″ x 10″ rectangle.

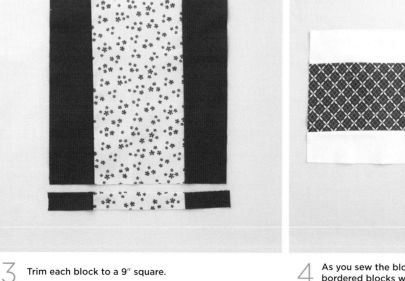

3 Trim each block to a 9″ square.

4 As you sew the blocks together, alternate the light bordered blocks with the dark bordered blocks. Notice the direction of the blocks alternates as well.

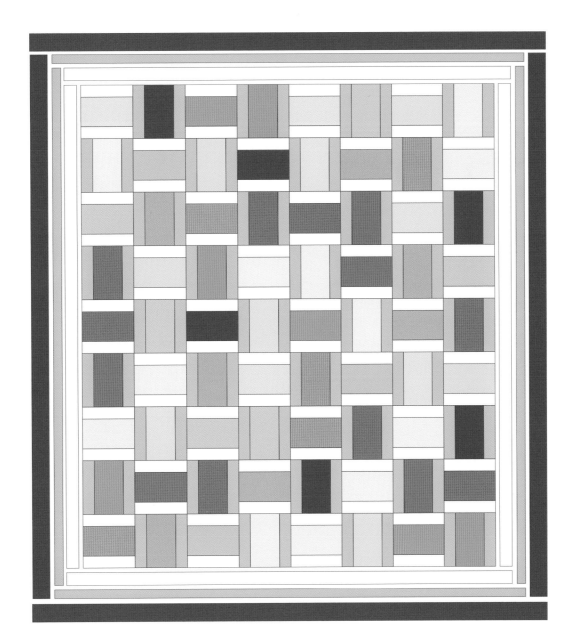

friendship star
sashing

quilt designed by JENNY DOAN

Life is busy. When my first baby was born, it seemed like suddenly every moment was filled to the brim with diaper changes, midnight feedings, and endless piles of laundry. Of course, I have countless precious memories from those days, but in frazzled, sleep-deprived moments, I sometimes thought to myself, "Won't it be nice when things get back to normal and I have a little time to myself?"

Soon we were blessed with another sweet baby, and then another. It wasn't long before we had a whole passel of kids running around the house, and the little time I had was stretched to the limit with carpools, Little League, piano lessons, and homework. And that pile of laundry produced by our small family of three? Oh, it grew by leaps and bounds! I think I've washed enough dirty socks in my lifetime to win some sort of award! On days when I was knee-deep in science fair projects and visits to the dentist, I'd think to myself, "Once these kids are grown and gone, I'll have so much free time; I just won't know what to do with myself."

For the tutorial and everything you need to make this quilt visit:
www.msqc.co/blocksummer16

56

Little did I know that life never really slows down. Each year the days seem to race by faster and faster and I find myself wondering how on earth January turned to June in the blink of an eye! Summertime, however, gives me a chance to stop and breathe and just enjoy the simple things.

We Doans make it a point to get together for family cookouts throughout the summer. Ron fires up the grill, I make my special cookies, the kids bring delicious salads and fresh fruit, and the grandchildren just run wild. After the meal is done, we sit on the porch and talk for hours on end. Even after the daylight has faded, we're not too worried about bedtime and schedules. After all, that's what summer's all about! Of course, I know that morning will bring a new set of challenges and demands, but as we sit together looking out over the cool, green grass at the setting sun, time seems to stand still and we are free to just be.

There's no sense in wishing for calmer days with fewer responsibilities. Time marches on and there are always a million tasks competing for our attention. So when something is truly important, you've simply got to make it happen. This summer, be sure to carve out a bit of time here and there to do what makes you happy. Allow yourself some time to focus on your quilting, to pamper yourself, and, most importantly, to connect with loved ones. After all, every moment we have on earth is a gift. Fill those moments with as much joy as you can!

materials

makes a 77" x 88½" quilt

QUILT TOP
- 1 package of 10" squares (42 ct.)
- 1½ yards background
- 1 yard contrasting solid

BORDER
- 1½ yards

BINDING
- ¾ yard

BACKING
- 7 yards

SAMPLE QUILT
- **Oh My Stars** by Dover Hill for Benartex

1 cut

From the background fabric, cut:

- (18) 2½" strips across the width of the fabric – subcut the strips into 10" rectangles for a **total of 71.**

From the contrasting solid fabric, cut:

- (11) 2½" strips across the width of the fabric – subcut the strips into 2½" squares for a **total of 172.**

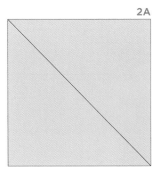

2A

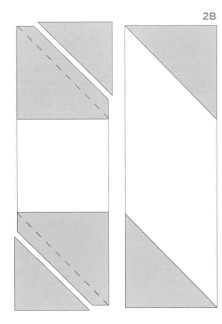

2B

2 block construction

On the reverse side of 142 contrasting solid 2½" squares, draw a line from corner to corner once on the diagonal. 2A

Place a contrasting solid square on either end of each background sashing rectangle. The squares should be oriented so the drawn line runs from upper left to the bottom right at one end of the rectangle and from bottom right to upper left on the other end. Sew on the drawn line, then trim the excess fabric ¼" away from the sewn seam. **Make 71.** 2B

Sew the 10" squares together in **rows of 6** with a background sashing rectangle between each block. **Make 7 rows.** 2C

4 border

Cut (8) 5½" strips across the width of the fabric. Sew the strips together end-to-end to make one long strip. Trim the borders from this strip.

Refer to Borders (pg. 100) in the Construction Basics to measure and cut the outer borders. The strips are approximately 79" for the sides and approximately 77½" for the top and bottom.

5 quilt and bind

Layer the quilt with backing and batting and quilt as desired. Square up and trim the excess batting and backing away. Add binding to finish. See the Construction Basics (pg. 101) for binding instructions.

2C

3 arrange rows

Make a sashing strip to go between each row of blocks. Each row begins and ends with a sashing rectangle and alternates with a contrasting solid square. **Make 6 rows.** 3A

3A

Sew the rows together alternating a block row with a sashing strip. 3B

1 Place a marked 2½″ contrasting square on either end of a 2½″ background rectangle with right sides facing. Sew on the marked line and trim ¼″ away from the sewn seam.

2 Sew the 10″ blocks together, adding a sashing rectangle between each square.

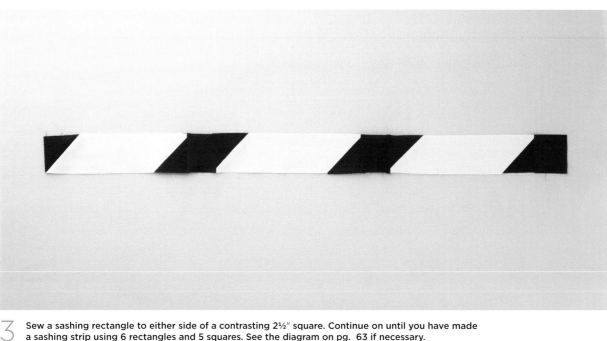

3 Sew a sashing rectangle to either side of a contrasting 2½″ square. Continue on until you have made a sashing strip using 6 rectangles and 5 squares. See the diagram on pg. 63 if necessary.

For the tutorial and everything you need to make this quilt visit:
www.msqc.co/blocksummer16

dandy stars

quilt designed by JENNY DOAN

I have seven children. Seven. And when you're talking about children, seven is basically the same thing as a hundred. When the kids were small and we'd walk to the library, I'm sure I looked like a mother duck leading her seven little ducklings along the path. We even had that one straggler who would get distracted by every shiny rock or creeping insect, fall behind, and then race his short little legs to catch up. It was quite the effort to get them there!

Trips to the grocery store were like a slapstick movie scene with one child knocking over a display of baked beans while another was trying to covertly slip a package of chocolate chip cookies into the cart, and still another sat right down in the middle of the cereal aisle, declaring loudly that she was too hungry and exhausted to continue. All I could do is shake my head and sigh.

Strangers reacted to our robust brood with everything from shock and disdain to pity for me, the poor weary mother of her own small army, but I paid them no mind. I knew something that they did not. Children are wonderful. So, it stands to reason that seven children are magnificent! My life was never dull or boring, and I never lacked for hugs and sticky little kisses. Did I enjoy every moment raising those seven little people? I'll plead the fifth on that one. But I tell

dandy stars quilt

ya, the good outweighed the bad by so much, looking back, that's really all I can remember!

Large families can be loud and expensive and, at times, chaotic, but they are a whole lot of fun as well! Every year when school let out for the summer, the kids would start begging to go to the park. After packing a little picnic we'd venture out for a day in the sun. One of our favorite things to do at the park was play baseball. Of course, we're not talking about a simple game of catch. When you have a big family like ours, you can orchestrate a full game complete with catcher, shortstop, and plenty of outfielders. This was the real deal.

I'll never forget the time Sarah hit her very first home run. She stood there on home plate, unsure if someone in the outfield would catch the ball or if she should drop her bat and run. Well, I was playing umpire, so I gave her a gentle nudge and told her to run like crazy! That girl took off like someone had lit a fire under her, toting the bat along the whole way. When she made it back to home plate, completely out of breath, the whole family had gathered there, waiting to give her a high five or a big hug. It filled my heart to the brim to hear everyone cheering for her. Then we dispatched a search party to find the ball out in the bushes around the field.

Now that our family has grown to include in-laws and many wonderful grandchildren, we still love to get together for a game of baseball. These days we have enough people for two full teams, fans on the bleachers, and even our own cute little cheerleaders on the sidelines. My heart swells with joy as I look around at the ever-expanding gaggle of Doans and shout, "Let's play ball!"

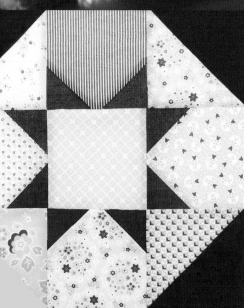

Here's another colorway of this block. Try different combinations of fabric to see which one you like best.

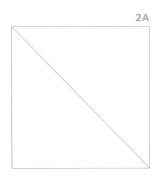

materials

makes a 49½" X 49½" quilt

QUILT TOP
- 3 packages of 5" print squares (42 ct.)
- 1¾ yards background

BINDING
- ½ yard

BACKING
- 3 yards

SAMPLE QUILT
- **Welcome Wagon** by Kim Diehl for Henry Glass

1 cut

From the background fabric, cut:

- (5) 5" strips across the width of the fabric. Subcut each strip into 5" squares. Each strip will yield 8 squares and you need a **total of 36.**

- (10) 2½" strips across the width of the fabric. Subcut the strips into 2½" squares. Each strip will yield 16 squares and you need a **total of 148.** Set **76 squares** aside for the border. The remainder will be used in the blocks.

2A

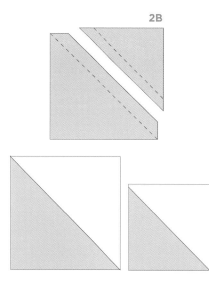

2B

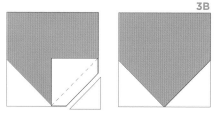

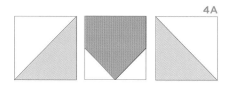

3A

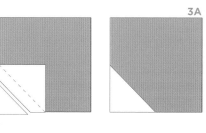

3B

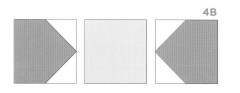

4A

4B

2 half-square triangles

Fold a 5″ background square from corner to corner once on the diagonal and press the crease in place. The crease will mark your sewing line. 2A

Layer a creased 5″ background square with a 5″ print square with right sides facing. Sew from corner to corner once on the crease. Move the block ½″ away from the sewn seam and sew another seam parallel with the first. Trim ¼″ away from the first sewn seam. **Make 4** large half-square triangle units and 4 small half-square triangles. Set the small units aside for another project. 2B

3 center units

Fold (8) 2½″ background squares from corner to corner once on the diagonal. Press the crease in place in each square to mark your sewing line. (See diagram 2A if necessary.) Place a 2½″ background square on one side of a print 5″ square with right sides facing. Stitch along the crease. Trim the excess fabric ¼″ away from the sewn seam. 3A

Place a 2½″ background square on the adjacent side of the 5″ print square with right sides facing. Again, sew on the

crease and trim the excess fabric ¼″ away from the sewn seam. **Make 4** of these center units. 3B

4 block construction

Sew a half-square triangle unit to either side of a center unit. **Make 2.** 4A

Sew a center unit to either side of a print square. **Make 1.** 4B

Sew the 3 rows together to complete the block. **Make 9 blocks.** 4C

Block Size: 13½″ x 13½″ finished

5 arrange and sew

Lay out the blocks in **3 rows** with each row containing **3 blocks.** Sew the rows together when you are happy with the layout.

6 border blocks

The border is made up of the same pieces we called the center units. Refer to those instructions and **make 36.**

You'll need to make 4 corner units for the border as well. Crease a 2½″ square to mark your sewing line. Place the square on one corner of a print 5″ square and sew on the crease. Trim the excess fabric away ¼″ from the sewn seam. 6A

4C

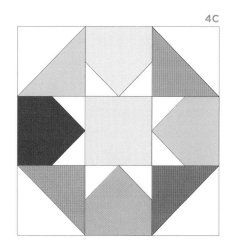

6A

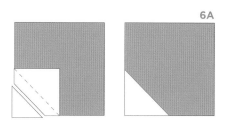

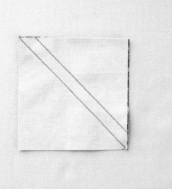

1 On the reverse side of a background 5″ square, mark a line from corner to corner once on the diagonal. Layer the square with a print square with right sides facing and sew on the marked line. Move the square out ½″ and sew another seam toward the outer edge.

2 Cut between the two sewn seams. You will have a large half-square triangle and a small half-square triangle. Set the small half-square triangles aside for another project.

3 Mark a 2½″ background square and place it on one corner of a 5″ print square. Sew on the marked line then trim ¼″ away from the sewn seam.

4 Repeat step 3 for the adjacent side of the print square.

5 Sew a half-square triangle unit to either side of a center unit. Make 2 rows in this manner.

6 Sew the three rows together to complete the block.

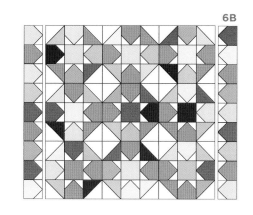

6B

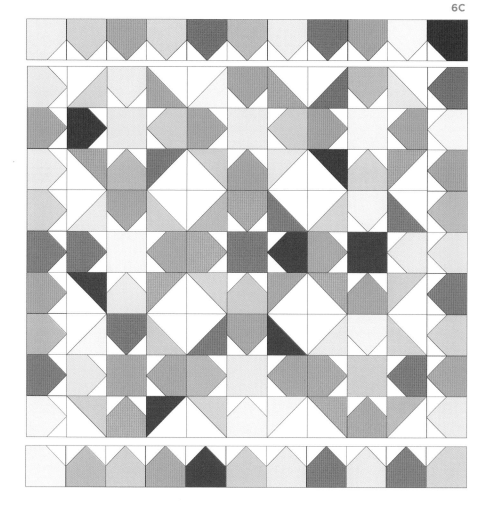

6C

Measure the quilt through the center in several places horizontally and vertically, staying at least 6″ away from the outer edges. You should have a measurement of approximately 41″ square.

Sew 9 center units together. The strip should measure the same as your quilt top. If it doesn't, make a few minor adjustments in the seam allowances, either using a scanter seam allowance or a more generous one. Spread adjustments out as much as possible and they won't be noticeable. Make 4 strips the same length as your measurement. Sew one strip to either side of the quilt. **6B**

Sew a corner unit to either end of the two remaining strips. Sew one strip to the top of the quilt and the other to the bottom. **6C**

7 quilt and bind

Layer the quilt with batting and backing and quilt. After the quilting is complete, square up the quilt and trim away all excess batting and backing. Add binding to complete the quilt. See Construction Basics (pg. 101) for binding instructions.

wallflower

quilt designed by NATALIE EARNHEART

Every quilt has a story to tell. Some have grass stains from summer picnics or the scent of woodsmoke after decades of camping trips, others, with frayed edges, have comforted sweet babies night after night. The Wallflower quilt tells a story near and dear to my heart. It's the story of a bond between a little girl and her grandmother.

The original Wallflower quilt was made for my daughter-in-law Misty by her grandmother. Like so many quilts, Misty's quilt is full of memories. Soon after this quilt was made for her, Misty's grandmother passed away, but it will forever stand as a tangible reminder of so many wonderful moments spent in the company of that remarkable woman. I asked Misty to share her story, and this is what she said:

"When I was a little girl, I spent every day I could with my Grandma Sandi. She was beautiful, talented, hardworking—and she was my very best friend. We had a lot of fun together sewing, shopping at antique stores and yard sales, and gardening. Each spring, she bought flats full of colorful blooms, and I worked alongside her, filling pots with soil and then carefully planting the beautiful flowers. After the work was done, Grandma would pour me a big glass of lemonade and we'd sit on the porch and just talk.

"My grandma was also an avid quilter. When I was twelve years old, she made me a wonderful quilt with flowers on it that shadowed each other. On one side of the block, the flower is in color on a white background, and the other side is just the opposite, a shadow of the first. Shortly after she made my quilt, she was diagnosed with cancer. She passed only a few months after she gave me that precious gift, and it's a treasure that I'll cherish

forever. Perhaps when she was choosing the pattern, she thought of the time we spent together planting flowers. All of those sweet memories spending time with Grandma come flooding back to me every time I cuddle up in my quilt.

"A few years ago I showed the quilt to my mother-in-law, Jenny, and she loved it too. When the Mini Orange Peel Template came out, she knew she would be able to remake it simply and share it with all of you. I love how it came out, and now my daughter has a quilt from her grandma just like mine."

Here's another colorway of this block. Try different combinations of fabric to see which one you like best.

materials

makes a 62" X 74½" quilt

QUILT TOP
- 1 package print 10" squares (42 ct.)
- 1 package background 10" squares (42 ct.)

BORDER
- 1 yard

BINDING
- ¾ yard

BACKING
- 4½ yards

ADDITIONAL SUPPLIES
- MSQC Mini Orange Peel Template
- 4 yards fusible web

SAMPLE QUILT
- **Bahama Breeze** by Maria Kalinowski for Kanvas Studios

1 layer and cut

Layer a print 10" square with a background 10" square with right sides facing. Cut in half to make 5" x 10" rectangles. As you cut, put them in 2 stacks, leaving the pieces layered. One stack will be used for the base of the blocks and one stack will be used for the petals.

Sew a 5" x 10" print rectangle to a background 5" x 10" background rectangle. **Make 42 base blocks. 1A**

Pick up the petal stack and cut the 5" x 10" rectangles in half, making 5" squares. Use one set of squares

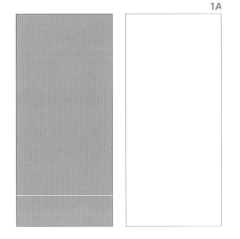

1A

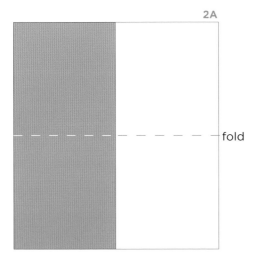

2A

fold

2B

2C

to make the petals and set the other aside for a different project.

Press the 5″ squares you're using for the petals onto the fusible web and cut:

- 3 petals from each square using the MSQC Mini Orange Peel template.

You need a **total of 252**, half will be of background fabric and half will be of prints. You might want to keep the print petals with the matching print background piece.

2 sew

Fold the block in half lengthwise and finger press a crease to mark the halfway point. **2A** Place 3 white petals on the print side of the block and 3 matching print petals on the background side of the block. Align the center petals with the crease and press in place. **2B** Add the petals on either side of the center petal, press and stitch in place using a small blanket stitch or, if you choose, a pretty decorative stitch. **Make 42 blocks.** 2C

Block Size: 9″ x 9½″ finished

Arrange the blocks in rows, keeping in mind that the blocks are rectangular rather than square. Make **7 rows** with each row having **6 blocks.** Press the seam allowances of the even numbered rows toward the right and the odd numbered rows toward the left. That will make your seam allowances nest.

3 border

Cut (7) 4½″ strips across the width of the fabric. Sew the strips together end-to-end to make one long strip. Trim the borders from this strip.

Refer to Borders (pg. 100) in the Construction Basics to measure and cut the outer borders. The strips are approximately 67″ for the sides and approximately 62½″ for the top and bottom.

4 quilt and bind

Layer the quilt with backing and batting and quilt as desired. Square up and trim the excess batting and backing away. Add binding to finish. See the Construction Basics (pg. 101) for binding instructions.

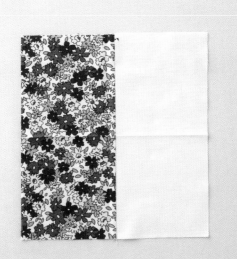

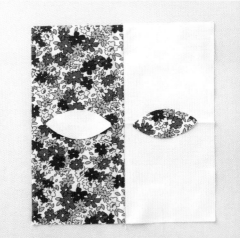

1 Sew a background 5″ x 10″ rectangle to a print 5″x 10″ rectangle. Make 42.

2 Press fusible web to the reverse side of the 5″ print squares and the 5″ background squares. Draw around the Mini Orange Peel Template and cut 3 petals from each fabric.

3 Place the print petals on the background side of the block and background petal on the other side and appliqué in place.

4 Sew the blocks together into rows, keeping in mind that you are working with rectangles rather than squares.

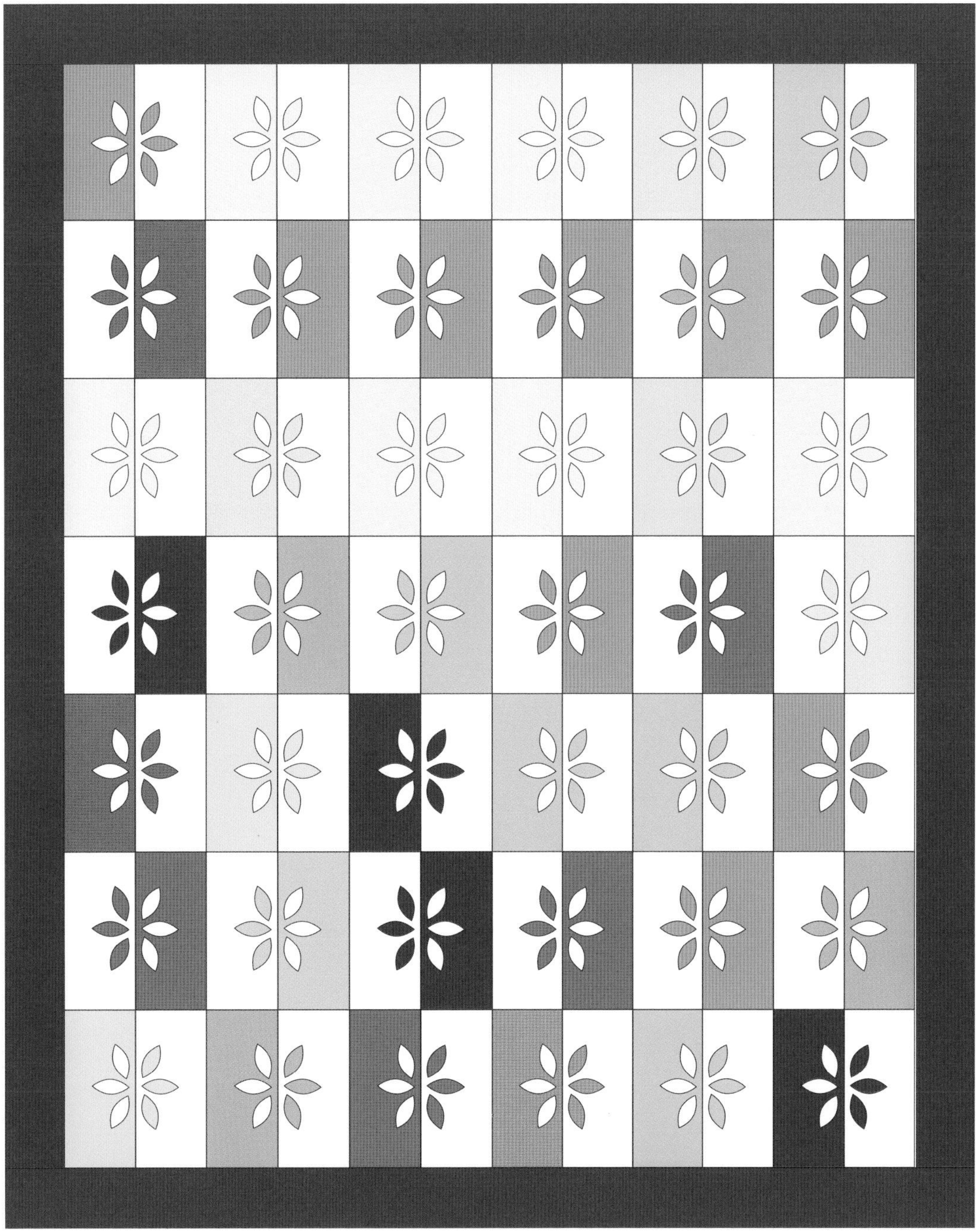

For the tutorial and everything you need to make this quilt visit:
www.msqc.co/blocksummer16

floating hexagons

quilt designed by JENNY DOAN

Have you ever heard someone tell a story that seemed so incredible, it just couldn't be real? In our family, when a story turns into a tall tale, we like to call it a "fish story," as in, "one time I caught a twenty-pound rainbow trout!" But I assure you, this is not one of those fish stories. This story doesn't require any embellishment.

When Ron was a small boy, one of his favorite things to do was go fishing with his dad. Fishing may not seem like the most lively activity. To the casual observer, it just looks like sitting in a boat with a pole in your hand, waiting, with little else going on. But for Ron, it's at the heart of his sweetest memories with his dad. He'll never forget their time together "teaching worms how to swim."

Ron must have told me a million times about one very eventful fishing trip with his dad. Full of excitement, they hastily launched their boat into the lake, but as it slid into the water, they suddenly realized that they'd forgotten to put the drain plug back into the bottom of the boat! Of course then the boat started to sink, as boats have a tendency to do when they fill up with water! Ron and his dad had no choice but to jump into the water and pull the boat out before it ended up at the bottom of the lake!

Instead of a lazy day of casting, reeling, and swapping exaggerated fishing tales, the guys ended up soaked to the bone and more than a little embarrassed. They might have been disappointed at the time but, you know, if they'd had a normal day of fishing it wouldn't have made for a very good story.

One of the things I enjoyed most about moving to Missouri was watching our family become true country folks, learning to live that slow-paced lifestyle. The kids blossomed here, spending their days carving out adventure and exploring the outdoors. They looked forward to warm weather every year so they could get back to the stream. I loved watching my kids go fishing with their dad, walking off to their favorite fishing spot with a tackle box in one hand and a fishing pole in the other. Now they have their own stories to tell of fishing with their dad.

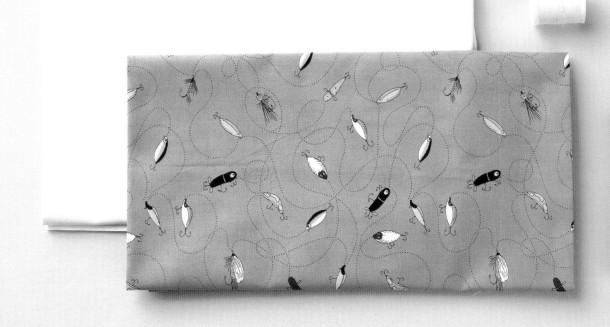

materials

makes a 56" X 78½" quilt

QUILT TOP
- 2 packages 5" (42 ct.) print squares
- 3 yards background (includes blocks, sashing and inner border)
- ¼ yard cornerstones

BORDER
- 1½ yards

BINDING
- ¾ yard

BACKING
- 5 yards

ADDITIONAL SUPPLIES
- 1 MSQC 5" Half-Hexagon Template

SAMPLE QUILT
- **Fishline** by Maywood

1 cut

Cut each 5" square in half. Place one piece atop the other with right sides facing. Place the Half-Hexagon Template on top of the 2 pieces. Using your rotary cutter, trim the edges even with the template. **1A**

From the background fabric, cut:

- (21) 2½" strips across the width of fabric.

- Subcut the strips into 2½" x 5" rectangles for a **total of 162**.

Stack 2 rectangles together with right sides facing. Place the Half-Hexagon Template on top of the 2 pieces. Using your rotary

1A

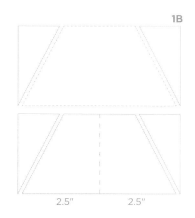

1B

2.5"   2.5"

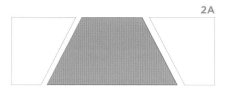

2A

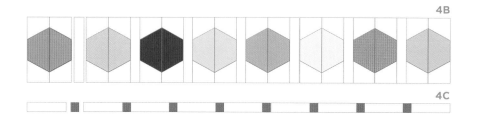

4B

4C

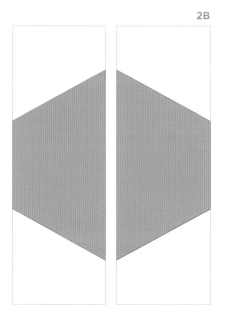

2B

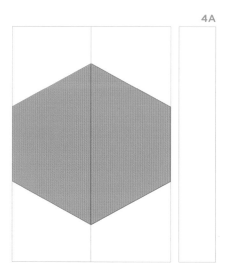

4A

cutter, trim the edges even with the template. Measure in from the outer edge and cut each of the half-hexagons in half, thus making a quarter-hexagon. **1B**

2 block construction

Sew a background quarter-hexagon to either side of a print hexagon with right sides facing. **Make 2** using matching prints. **2A**

Sew the two pieces together with right sides facing to complete the block. **Make 81**. **2B**

Block Size: 4" x 6½" finished

3 cut sashing strips and cornerstones

From the background fabric, cut:

- (21) 1½" strips across the width of the fabric.

- Subcut 12 strips into 1½" x 7" rectangles for a **total of 72**. Subcut the remaining 9 strips into 1½" x 4½" rectangles for a **total of 72**.

From the cornerstone fabric, cut:

- (3) 1½" strips across the width of the fabric.

- Subcut the strips into 1½" squares for a total of **64 squares**.

4 arrange blocks

Lay out and arrange the blocks to your satisfaction into 9 rows of 9 blocks. Sew a 1½" x 7" sashing strip between each of the blocks vertically, then sew each row together. **4A 4B**

Make 8 rows of horizontal sashing. Sew a 1½" x 4½" background rectangle to a 1½" cornerstone. Continue on in this manner until you have sewn 8 cornerstones in place, then end the row with a 1½" x 4½" rectangle. **4C**

Sew the rows together alternating a horizontal row of blocks with a row of horizontal sashing.

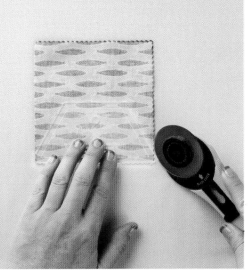

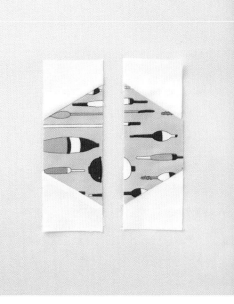

1 Using the MSQC Half-Hexagon Template, cut 2 pieces from each print square.

2 Cut background half-hexagon pieces in half again to make quarter hexagons

3 Sew 2 matching half-hexagon units together to complete the block.

4 Sew the blocks together. Notice that the sashing rectangles are only sewn between the blocks.

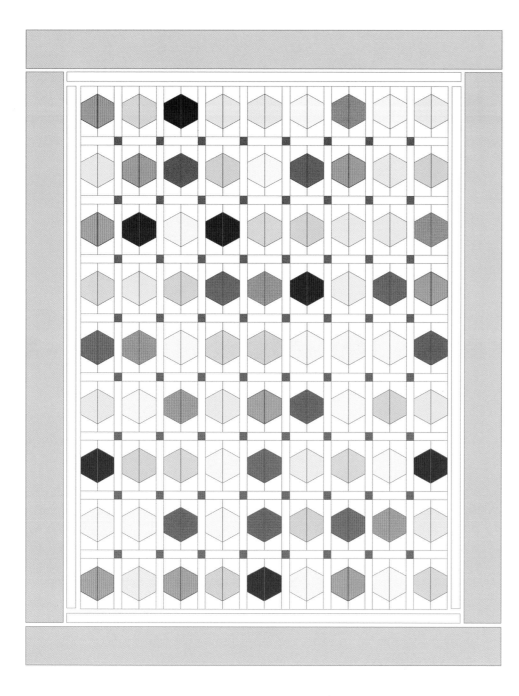

5 inner border

Cut (6) 1½" strips across the width of the fabric. Sew the strips together end-to-end to make one long strip. Trim the borders from this strip.

Refer to Borders (pg. 100) in the Construction Basics to measure and cut the inner borders. The strips are approximately 67" for the sides and approximately 46½" for the top and bottom.

6 outer border

Cut (7) 5½" strips across the width of the fabric. Sew the strips together end-to-end to make one long strip. Trim the borders from this strip.

Refer to Borders (pg. 100) in the Construction Basics to measure and cut the inner borders. The strips are approximately 69" for the sides and approximately 56½" for the top and bottom.

7 quilt and bind

Layer the quilt with batting and backing and quilt. After the quilting is complete, square up the quilt and trim away all excess batting and backing. Add binding to complete the quilt. See Construction Basics (pg. 101) for binding instructions.

a quilty proposal

We have a lot to be grateful for here at Missouri Star Quilt Co. What began as one longarm quilting machine in a little red brick store has blossomed far beyond what we ever could have imagined! But we recently added something pretty awesome to our list of accomplishments: a wedding! We aren't match makers, but from the introduction to the wedding day, we'd like to think we had a hand in helping this great couple get together.

Stephen met Sarah on his first day of work at one of our shops here in Hamilton. He found out that Sarah would be his trainer, which he didn't mind at all. After some time, they realized that they had taken a shine to each other, but guys don't always pick up on hints well. After some subtle flirting—which wasn't really getting through—Sarah bravely asked Stephen if he'd been dating anyone. Then it dawned on him that she was truly interested and he asked her on a date to the Renaissance Festival.

But before they even went out on that first date, Stephen joined Sarah for Sunday dinner to meet her parents. How proper! Then for their date the following day, he showed up with a rose and ice cream—the fastest way to a woman's heart, of course! Sarah couldn't help herself and she teased Stephen by hitting him with a foam sword saying, "I've been hitting on you all day so I thought maybe I could switch it up a little!" Now she'd found the way to his heart too. What guy can resist humor and beauty?!

the quilt during a retreat where he was welcomed with open arms! The ladies at the retreat loved having him there and offered plenty of support, advice, and motivation. He also received a lot of help from his coworkers: Cindy, Susan, Meg, and Glenda. Thanks ladies! Armed with some of the best tools in the business, Stephen finished the quilt top in just one week!

So on the morning of the company breakfast, with his heart in his throat, Stephen gathered up the special quilt and got down on one knee in front of everyone. The proposal was definitely a surprise and Sarah didn't have a clue—she even showed up to breakfast in her pajamas with messy hair! Luckily, she had a pair of jeans stashed in the car, which Stephen kindly talked her into wearing at the last minute. And of course she said yes.

In return for the quilt Stephen made, Sarah then made one for Stephen, only this one was big enough for two. The happy couple was married on March 4, 2016 and because MSQC is where it all started, it was only fitting that they celebrated with a reception in our beautiful Sewing Center! All's well that ends well and we're so glad we could be a part of this sweet love story.

If you couldn't guess, they were great together from the beginning. After that first date, Stephen immediately asked Sarah's mother for permission to take her on another date that same week. Being the smart guy that he is, he took her out for ice cream that Saturday, and that's when he really stole her heart.

It wasn't too long before they started talking about marriage. When it's right, it's right! They knew it was what they both wanted, but they just didn't know when.

So when the day finally came to propose, Stephen wanted to make it really special. And he knew just what to do. You can't work in a quilter's paradise without it rubbing off on you, so Stephen gathered up his determination and decided to make Sarah a quilt and surprise her with it at the company breakfast.

Despite a busy schedule working full time at the quilt shop and attending school full time too, Stephen made time to finish the quilt for Sarah. He even worked on

dandy
stars

QUILT SIZE
49½" X 49½"

DESIGNED BY
Jenny Doan

PIECED BY
Carol Henderson

QUILTED BY
James Evensen

QUILT TOP
3 packages of 5" print squares
  (42 ct.)
1¾ yards background

BINDING
½ yard

BACKING
3 yards

SAMPLE QUILT
Welcome Wagon by Kim Diehl
  for Henry Glass

ONLINE TUTORIALS
msqc.co/blocksummer16

QUILTING
Posies

PATTERN
pg. 64

dresden botanica

QUILT SIZE
65" X 78½"

DESIGNED BY
Jenny Doan

PIECED BY
Carol Henderson

QUILTED BY
Linda Frump

QUILT TOP
6 packages 5" squares
3 yards 42" wide background fabric

BORDER
1½ yards

BINDING
¾ yard

BACKING
4¾ yards

ADDITIONAL SUPPLIES
MSQC Dresden Plate Template
1 cardboard circle template cut from
    the template given on pg. 15.

SAMPLE QUILT
Bread and Butter by American
    Jane for Moda

ONLINE TUTORIALS
msqc.co/blocksummer16

QUILTING
Curly Twirly Flowers

PATTERN
pg. 8

floating hexagons

QUILT SIZE
56" X 78½"

DESIGNED BY
Jenny Doan

PIECED BY
Cindy Morris

QUILTED BY
Debbie Elder

QUILT TOP
2 packages 5" (42 ct.) print squares
3 yards background (includes blocks,
   sashing and inner border)
¼ yard cornerstones

BORDER
1½ yards

BINDING
¾ yard

BACKING
5 yards

ADDITIONAL SUPPLIES
1 MSQC 5" Half-Hexagon Template

SAMPLE QUILT
Fishline by Maywood

ONLINE TUTORIALS
msqc.co/blocksummer16

QUILTING
Posies

PATTERN
pg. 80

friendship star sashing

QUILT SIZE
77" X 88½"

DESIGNED BY
Jenny Doan

PIECED BY
Carol Henderson

QUILTED BY
Janet Caselman

QUILT TOP
1 package of 10" squares (42 ct.)
1½ yards background
1 yard contrasting solid

BORDER
1½ yards

BINDING
¾ yard

BACKING
7 yards

SAMPLE QUILT
Oh My Stars by Dover Hill for
   Benartex

ONLINE TUTORIALS
msqc.co/blocksummer16

QUILTING
Stars and Loops

PATTERN
pg. 56

I spy jar

QUILT SIZE
50″ X 63½″

DESIGNED BY
Jenny Doan

PIECED BY
Carol Henderson

QUILTED BY
Kara Snow

QUILT TOP
1 package 5″ squares (42 ct.)
¼ yard solid (lids)
2 yards background (includes inner
  border)

BORDER
1 yard

BINDING
¾ yard

BACKING
4 yards

SAMPLE QUILT
I Spy - It's A Boy Thing by Timeless
  Treasures

ONLINE TUTORIALS
msqc.co/blocksummer16

QUILTING
Loops and Swirls

PATTERN
pg. 16

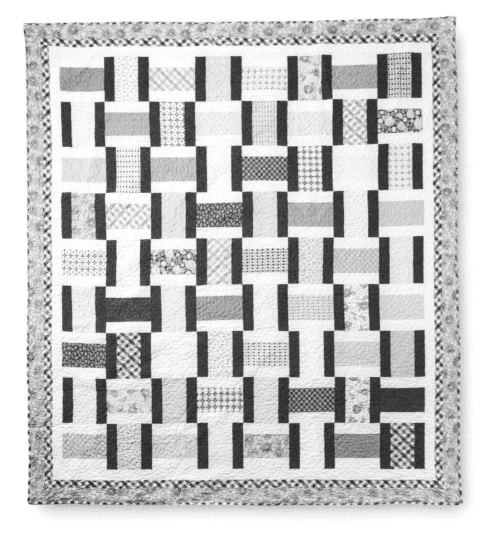

jelly basket

QUILT SIZE
81" X 89"

DESIGNED BY
Natalie Earnheart

PIECED BY
Cindy Morris

QUILTED BY
Devin Ragle

QUILT TOP
1 package 10" squares
2 yards light solid – includes inside
   border
1½ yards dark solid

MIDDLE BORDER
¾ yard

OUTER BORDER
1 yard

BINDING
¾ yard

BACKING
7½ yards

SAMPLE QUILT
Summerfest by April Rosenthal
   for Moda

ONLINE TUTORIALS
msqc.co/blocksummer16

QUILTING
Meander

QUILT PATTERN
pg. 48

rhombus
cube

QUILT SIZE
80" X 80¾"

DESIGNED BY
Natalie Earnheart

PIECED BY
Cindy Morris

QUILTED BY
Debbie Elder

QUILT TOP
2 yards light
2 yards medium
2 yards dark
1½ yards solid (we used gray) -
    includes yardage for border

BACKING
7½ yards

BINDING
¾ yard

OTHER SUPPLIES
MSQC Rhombus Template

SAMPLE QUILT
Kona Solids: Titanium K00-500,
    Pool K00-45 *OR* **Azure** K00-1009,
    Nightfall K00-140, **Aqua** K00-1005

ONLINE TUTORIALS
msqc.co/blocksummer16

QUILTING
City Windows

QUILT PATTERN
pg. 40

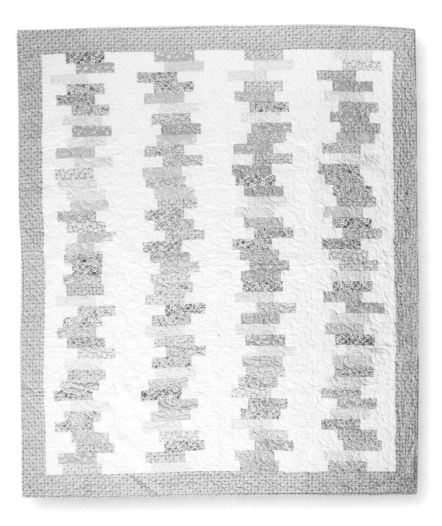

stacks

QUILT SIZE
76½" X 89"

DESIGNED BY
Jenny Doan

PIECED BY
Carol Henderson

QUILTED BY
Kara Snow

QUILT TOP
1 roll print 2½" strips
1 roll background strips

BORDER
1½ yards

BINDING
¾ yard

BACKING
7 yards

SAMPLE QUILT
Pinafores and Petticoats by Kaye
  England for Wilmington Prints

ONLINE TUTORIALS
msqc.co/blocksummer16

QUILTING
Champagne Bubbles

PATTERN
pg. 26

summer in the park

QUILT SIZE
74" X 81¾"

DESIGNED BY
Natalie Earnheart

PIECED BY
Cindy Morris

QUILTED BY
Janet Caselman

QUILT TOP
1 roll of 2½" print strips
1 roll of 2½" background strips

INNER BORDER
¾ yard

OUTER BORDER AND BINDING
1¾ yards

BACKING
5 yards

SAMPLE QUILT
Blossom Batiks Jewel Tones by
  Flaurie & Finch for RJR

ONLINE TUTORIALS
msqc.co/blocksummer16

QUILTING
Wind Swirls

PATTERN
pg. 32

wallflower

QUILT SIZE
62" X 74½"

DESIGNED BY
Jenny Doan

PIECED BY
Carol Henderson

QUILTED BY
Linda Frump

QUILT TOP
1 package print 10" squares (42 ct.)
1 package background 10" squares
  (42 ct.)

BORDER
1 yard

BINDING
¾ yard

BACKING
4½ yards

ADDITIONAL SUPPLIES
MSQC Mini Orange Peel Template
4 yards fusible web

SAMPLE QUILT
Bahama Breeze by Maria Kalinowski
  for Kanvas Studios

ONLINE TUTORIALS
msqc.co/blocksummer16

QUILTING
Loops & Swirls

PATTERN
pg. 72

construction basics

- All seams are ¼" inch unless directions specify differently.

- Cutting instructions are given at the point when cutting is required.

- Precuts are not prewashed; therefore do not prewash other fabrics in the project

- All strips are cut WOF

- Remove all selvages

- All yardages based on 42" WOF

ACRONYMS USED

MSQC	Missouri Star Quilt Co.
RST	right sides together
WST	wrong sides together
HST	half-square triangle
WOF	width of fabric
LOF	length of fabric

pre-cut glossary

5" SQUARE PACK

1 = (42) 5" squares or ¾ yd of fabric
1 = baby
2 = crib
3 = lap
4 = twin

2½" STRIP ROLL

1 = (40) 2½" strip roll cut the width of fabric
    or 2¾ yds of fabric
1 = a twin
2 = queen

10" SQUARE PACK

1 = (42) 10" square pack of fabric: 2¾ yds total
1 = a twin
2 = queen

When we mention a precut, we are basing the pattern on a 40-42 count pack. Not all precuts have the same count, so be sure to check the count on your precut to make sure you have enough pieces to complete your project.

general quilting

- All seams are ¼" inch unless directions specify differently.
- Cutting instructions are given at the point when cutting is required.
- Precuts are not prewashed; therefore do not prewash other fabrics in the project.
- All strips are cut width of fabric.
- Remove all selvages.
- All yardages based on 42" width of fabric (WOF).

press seams

- Use the cotton setting on your iron when pressing.
- Press the seam just as it was sewn RST. This "sets" the seam.
- To set the seam, press just as it was sewn with right sides together.
- With dark fabric on top, lift the dark fabric and press back.
- The seam allowance is pressed toward the dark side. Some patterns may direct otherwise for certain situations.
- Press toward borders. Pieced borders may demand otherwise.
- Press diagonal seams open on binding to reduce bulk.

borders

- Always measure the quilt top 3 times before cutting borders.
- Start measuring about 4" in from each side and through the center vertically.
- Take the average of those 3 measurements.
- Cut 2 border strips to that size. Piece strips together if needed.
- Attach one to either side of the quilt.
- Position the border fabric on top as you sew. The feed dogs can act like rufflers. Having the border on top will prevent waviness and keep the quilt straight.
- Repeat this process for the top and bottom borders, measuring the width 3 times.
- Include the newly attached side borders in your measurements.
- Press toward the borders.

binding

find a video tutorial at: www.msqc.co/006

- Use 2½" strips for binding.
- Sew strips end-to-end into one long strip with diagonal seams, aka plus sign method (next). Press seams open.
- Fold in half lengthwise wrong sides together and press.
- The entire length should equal the outside dimension of the quilt plus 15" - 20."

plus sign method

- Lay one strip across the other as if to make a plus sign right sides together.
- Sew from top inside to bottom outside corners crossing the intersections of fabric as you sew. Trim excess to ¼" seam allowance.
- Press seam open.

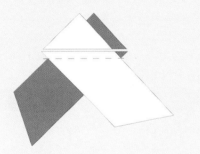

attach binding

- Match raw edges of folded binding to the quilt top edge.
- Leave a 10" tail at the beginning.
- Use a ¼" seam allowance.
- Start in the middle of a long straight side.

find a video tutorial at: www.msqc.co/001

10" tail ¼"

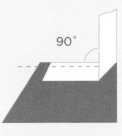

90° fold

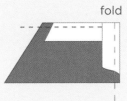

miter corners

- Stop sewing ¼" before the corner.
- Move the quilt out from under the presser foot.
- Clip the threads.
- Flip the binding up at a 90° angle to the edge just sewn.
- Fold the binding down along the next side to be sewn, aligning raw edges.
- The fold will lie along the edge just completed.
- Begin sewing on the fold.

close binding

*MSQC recommends **The Binding Tool** from TQM Products to finish binding perfectly every time.*

- Stop sewing when you have 12" left to reach the start.
- Where the binding tails come together, trim excess leaving only 2½" of overlap.
- It helps to pin or clip the quilt together at the two points where the binding starts and stops. This takes the pressure off of the binding tails while you work.
- Use the plus sign method to sew the two binding ends together, except this time when making the plus sign, match the edges. Using a pencil, mark your sewing line because you won't be able to see where the corners intersect. Sew across.

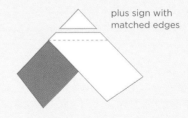

plus sign with matched edges

- Trim off excess; press seam open.
- Fold in half wrong sides together, and align all raw edges to the quilt top.
- Sew this last binding section to the quilt. Press.
- Turn the folded edge of the binding around to the back of the quilt and tack into place with an invisible stitch or machine stitch if you wish.

THE FAIR THIEF

PART 2
Techno-Quilty

A JENNY DOAN MYSTERY

written by Steve Westover

Outside the restaurant, MK took a look at Stephanie's candy apple red Mini Cooper parked alongside the curb. MK folded her arms and looked to Jenny in protest, "She's kidding, right?"

Jenny shrugged her shoulders, grinned, and then said, "Stephanie, it's adorable. I love the racing stripe!"

"And where do you propose that I sit?" MK asked.

Stephanie's eyes narrowed but she didn't respond. She climbed in the driver's seat, started the tiny car, and waited, "Don't be a baby. Climb in!"

"How?" MK huffed.

"I have confidence in you, MK. You'll figure it out," Jenny said, suppressing a chuckle.

MK slid the passenger side seat forward as far as she could and shoved a suitcase, duffle bag, blanket, and vacuum cleaner out of her way. She crammed herself sideways into the back seat but didn't buckle the seat belt because she couldn't find it ... or move her arms.

Jenny set the passenger seat into its normal position and winced when she heard MK squeal in temporary pain. "Sorry!"

"Where to?" Stephanie asked.

"The crime scene, of course."

"And make it snappy," MK added from the rear.

Stephanie checked her mirrors and abruptly slammed the gas pedal to the floor. The Mini Cooper blasted from it's parking space and into traffic, forcing Jenny to grab the panic bar above her window with both hands. Stephanie weaved between cars and somehow made it through a traffic signal on the sixth second of a yellow light.

Arriving at the fairgrounds in world record time, Stephanie bounced out of her seat while Jenny reluctantly peeled her fingers from the bar. MK's rigid body slid from the backseat as she tried to keep her breakfast in her stomach where it belonged.

MK's lips puckered and her eyelids fluttered. "Never again," she said softly, "NEVER. AGAIN."

Jenny and MK rushed to keep up with Stephanie's impossibly fast gait as the woman practically sprinted toward the circus tent where the quilting competition had concluded the day before. Most of the quilts were still displayed for fairgoers to admire but there were noticeable gaps where a few quilters had removed their work and headed home early and, of course, where the winning quilts had been before they were stolen. But there was no police tape. No evidence of police involvement at all. To the average patron enjoying the quilted artwork, it would be impossible to recognize that anything had gone wrong.

Jenny examined the entryway to the tent, which was essentially a heavy flap of vinyl pulled out and staked into a canopy over the entrance. When pulled down, the vinyl entrance would only be sealed by three ties of thin rope on each side. "It's not hard to imagine how the thief gained entrance," Jenny said.

"Yeah, my eight-year-old nephew could get past those ties," Stephanie added.

Jenny took a step outside the tent to survey her surroundings. In the distance she could see the Tilt-A-Whirl and hear children screaming as it climbed and twisted into the air. In the foreground of the ride was a snack shack topped by a plain white sign with large printed letters reading "FRIED TREATS." *Ambiguous and somewhat frightening*, Jenny thought. To her left was a shaved ice booth and an artist's tent where a gray-haired, beret-wearing man spray painted caricatures of his customers, and to the right, a small petting zoo with goats and a pony.

"The fair planners didn't do a whole lot of planning, did they?" MK suggested.

"It's a little chaotic, for sure," Jenny agreed. "But chaos

is part of the experience, isn't it?" She thought about the question for a moment before she walked over to the artist's booth. She watched with interest as he finished spray painting the portrait of a man with a ridiculously large chin. She peeked around the shop where his other art was displayed for sale. "Business good?" Jenny asked. The man nodded and continued painting. Then she added, "See anything strange lately?"

"We're at the fair," the man replied.

"Good point," Jenny said as she strolled away from the booth. She stood still and then turned in place soaking in the chaos: the smells, the sounds, the electricity of the crowd. "It's a perfect place for crime," she muttered to herself.

Jenny snapped out of her thoughts when she heard Stephanie's familiar shrill voice yelling her name. "JENNY!" Stephanie joined her as an older woman trailed behind. "Jenny, you remember Beatrice, don't you?"

Jenny examined the approaching woman as MK leaned in and whispered in her ear, "She's the first place winner."

"Of course, I remember Beatrice." Jenny winked at MK and then waited a moment for Beatrice to catch up and join them. Beatrice looked like the prototypical grandmother—her short gray hair had a tinge of blond and she wore an oversized brooch like a nametag. "I'm so sorry about your gorgeous quilt," Jenny offered. "We're doing our best to help you find it."

"Thank you," Beatrice said. "That quilt is very important to me. It breaks my heart to think someone else could display it as if it were their own, or even copy it."

"It's terrible," Jenny agreed.

"I'm hoping to publish a quilting book with some of my designs and that one is my favorite. But now ..."

"Beatrice, do you have the design for the quilt?" Stephanie asked.

"Of course. It's at home."

Stephanie smiled. "Perfect. I want you to protect your ownership of the design. When you get home, make a copy of the design, write the date on it, and then mail it to yourself. When you receive it in the mail, don't open it. It will have a postal date stamped on it which will establish that no one could have created the same pattern after you mailed it to yourself. It will work like a copyright. Does that make sense?"

Beatrice looked confused but she nodded anyway.

Jenny shook her head. "I'm sorry Stephanie, but it doesn't work that way. I wish it were that simple."

Stephanie's tinny voice raised an octave even though she tried to remain calm, "Why doesn't it work that way, Jenny?"

After a moment's thought, Jenny explained, "Well, first, you have to ensure that the design is truly original. That can be hard to do because there are so many quilts out there and altering an existing pattern doesn't mean a design is original. It can be a little complicated."

"But I didn't copy anything," Beatrice said.

"I understand, Beatrice. And I'm not saying you did. Your design may be perfectly unique. I really couldn't say for sure, but if you're thinking about publishing the design in a book, you may want to talk to a copyright lawyer."

MK coughed and looked toward the ground. Then, leaning towards Jenny said, "Are you trying to scare the poor woman? Lawyers aren't very comforting."

Jenny took a deep breath and then looked Beatrice in the eye. "I'm sorry Beatrice. I'm not trying to dissuade you, but I do want you to understand that if you want to copyright your design, you need to do it the proper way and sending it to yourself in the mail, although well-intentioned, doesn't work."

"What should I do?" Beatrice asked.

"At the very least, you need to register the design at the U.S. Copyright Office. If you give me your email I'll have MK send you the link and some information," Jenny offered.

Beatrice stood there stunned, unsure of what to say or think.

Jenny stepped toward Beatrice and then wrapped her arms around her. "Don't worry. Everything is going to work out. Don't be overwhelmed."

"Besides, we're going to find your quilt," MK added. "Right?"

"Of course," Stephanie said.

Jenny's eyebrows rose into her bangs. "MK, please get Beatrice's email and phone number so we can keep in touch. And Beatrice, I'd be happy to take a look at your book when you're ready to publish. In the meantime, do everything you can to copyright your quilt designs and we'll do everything we can to find the quilt and that rotten thief."

Beatrice hugged Jenny again. "You are such a sweet young lady. Thank you."

"Young lady. Ha!" MK chortled.

"Please let me know what you find out." A tear gathered in the corner of Beatrice's eye as she turned to walk away.

"We will," MK called out. Jenny, MK, and Stephanie watched Beatrice stroll out of sight.

"What now, Jenny?" Stephanie asked.

"Yeah, what's our next move?" MK added enthusiastically.

Jenny racked her brain for a plan. Anything. After a moment of silence she closed her eyes and rubbed her temples. Then she admitted, "I have no idea."

The smiles, hope, and enthusiasm fell from MK's and Stephanie's faces as if Jenny had slapped them both. The confusion was palpable. Jenny felt their disappointment.

But before she could feel too badly, she heard the buzz of toy drones and noticed two mini-helicopters flying about forty feet overhead. They seemed to be racing as they dipped toward a tent and then rose higher into the air. Without taking her eyes off of the drones, she followed. "Jenny!" She heard someone call her name but paid no heed.

People in Jenny's path moved aside to avoid collision as she chased down the toy aircraft. The drones then lowered out of sight somewhere between the FRIED TREATS shack and the Tilt-A-Whirl. Jenny hurried to the open-air booth where two vendors controlled the toy aircrafts. Teenage boys had gathered around, impressed by the aerial display but Jenny ended the fun.

"I have a question," she said, walking directly to the older of the two vendors. She didn't wait for a response or any acknowledgement. "How do you fly those in areas where you can't see?" She realized the question sounded goofy so she tried to rephrase. "How are you able to fly your drones if you don't have a line of sight?"

The vendor lifted a drone from the table and showed Jenny the underside. "Camera." He then set it down and picked up a large controller with a monitor at the center and showed her. "Video display."

"Do they record?" Jenny asked.

The vendor could feel a sale coming on. "Sure. These models can be programed to record up to thirty minutes."

"Is that all?"

Just as quickly as the sale appeared, it seemed to be slipping away. Another vendor, who looked to be a freshman in high school, stepped in to save the day. "But ... if you're interested in recording time, we have security drones that can transmit the recordings to a DVR for up to 12 hours. Look at this one." He pulled out a round drone that looked like a flying saucer from a locked cabinet. "What's cool is you can program this one to hover so you don't have to continuously control it."

"Jenny, what are you ...?" MK started asking but Jenny cut her off.

"Look at this MK. It's a security drone. It can hover and record for up to 12 hours."

MK's head tilted. "So what?"

Jenny turned back to the pimply freshman. "Please tell me you use a security drone to protect your merchandise and booth at night."

The young kid looked unsure about whether or not he should answer, so Jenny asked again, "Please. It's important. Did you have a drone hovering last night, recording for security purposes?"

The older vendor shrugged his shoulders, so the freshman answered. He swallowed hard and then cleared his throat. He whispered, "Yes."

Jenny's face brightened as her smile reached from ear to ear. "Can I buy that drone and the recording? I'll throw in a little extra for your commission," Jenny offered.

"SOLD!" the older man said.

Turning to MK, Jenny said, "I have an idea."